ADVANCE

"While Lindkvist's ideas are anything but small, this blurb can be tiny: This Is Great."

Ben Hammersley, RSA Fellow, *Wired* journalist, Internet Visionary and author of *Approaching the Future: 64 Things You Need to Know Now for Then*

"Magnus Lindkvist is not only a world-class trendspotter and a futurologist with uncommonly deep insights into the shape of things to come, he is also a highly original thinker. In this *Minifesto* he has condensed a remarkable amount of challenging and contrarian thinking into a rousing defense of small, but not insignificant, ideas. It is a refreshing attack on pompous futures thinking and overly broad claims regarding the future, and champions humility and creativity in the face of the profoundly unknowable. An important book for all those who care about the world tomorrow."

Professor Alf Rehn, innovation thought-leader, listed on the 2016 Thinkers50 Radar as one of the "30 management thinkers most likely to shape the future of how organizations are managed and led".

"In *Minifesto* Magnus Lindkvist takes us on an unpredictable journey, where we discover how small things in life can help us explore big ideas that can create our future."

Stefan Engeseth, author of *Sharkonomics*
and Guest Professor

"This is simultaneously a simple and complex read, but necessary for any CEO who can't forecast the future but wants to understand how tomorrow is shaped today. The value of Lindkvist's Minifesto is not what is written, but what you will think about after you have read it. To make it scalable read it again after a few weeks. I did. Recommended reading on an 8 hour flight. 2 hours to read, 6 hours at 30.000ft."

Michael Setterdahl, Former CEO of Nucor Trading

"Not another book about a revolutionary new idea that will change everything. This is a great reminder that a weekend in Venice is nice but all those Mondays in between highlights are the foundation for a strong relationship. *Minifesto* is the concept for innovation when the speed of change makes anything big too slow. Mignificent!"

Stefan Hyttfors, futurist and author of *Yoga for Leaders*

MINIFESTO

WHY **SMALL IDEAS** MATTER IN THE
WORLD OF **GRAND NARRATIVES**

Published by
LID Publishing Ltd.
One Adam Street, London. WC2N 6LE

31 West 34th Street, 8th Floor, Suite 8004
New York, NY 10001, US

info@lidpublishing.com
www.lidpublishing.com

A member of:

BPR
Business Publishers Roundtable

www.businesspublishersroundtable.com

Printed in the Czech Republic by Finidr
ISBN: 978-1-910649-56-5

Cover and page design: Caroline Li

MINIFESTO

WHY **SMALL IDEAS** MATTER IN THE
WORLD OF **GRAND NARRATIVES**

MAGNUS
LINDKVIST

LONDON   MONTERREY
MADRID   SHANGHAI
MEXICO CITY BOGOTA
NEW YORK   BUENOS AIRES
BARCELONA   SAN FRANCISCO

CONTENTS

Preamble: *The Magic Mountain*   8

Introduction: Where does the future come from?   12

Chapter 1: Blanket-bombed by Blah-blah   18

Chapter 2: Welcome to The Seceity   32

Chapter 3: The Moment of Creation   46

Chapter 4: The Difference Between Ideas and Ideas   56

Chapter 5: Failureology   76

Chapter 6: Souvenirs From The Great Beyond   92

Chapter 7: Seeing What Could Be   108

Chapter 8: We-deas   126

Chapter 9: Blissful Ignorance   142

Chapter 10: Conclusion – The Unseen   156

Chapter ∞: The Minifesto   166

Sources   172

PREAMBLE

THE MAGIC MOUNTAIN

The top of the mountain is covered in snow that is slowly turning from icy blue to a radiant orange. The sun is rising and its rays are reaching over the Alps for the first time this morning. I am in the Swiss mountains to unwind, relax, seek refuge and reconnect with things lost. The word "vacation" has so often come to mean crowded airports, whining children and questionable hotel buffets that I have forgotten its etymological origin – to vacate. To leave something behind. To blow dust off the soul.

So here I am on a cold January morning with only the quiet whirr of the ski lift to accompany my thoughts and the view, which is nearly indescribable to those that haven't been there. Words like beautiful and heavenly have been ruined by abundant social media commentary – "You look so beautiful!" and "The cappuccino is heavenly!" – that to use them when describing this landscape would be to taint it slightly. Silence is more powerful. And when I hop off the ski lift and stand on top of the world, the silence is deafening. It is as if I can hear the blood flow in my veins. Like I exist in a state of equilibrium between a silence pressing inwards and the blood pressure outwards.

Like I don't exist.

Who am I? If we leave behind superficial traits like gender – male – and age – early 40s – I am a trendspotting futurologist. I spend my time thinking about change, in the world and its markets, industries and nations. I travel extensively. Too much, actually. Being a father of two young boys, I have spent far too many days and nights with my rear firmly parked on the faux-leather, flame-resistant upholstery of airplane seats. That's why I need a refuge. Inspired by a book called *The Magic Mountain*, I find myself in Davos, Switzerland.

The Magic Mountain – Der Zauberberg – by Thomas Mann was published in the mid-1920s between two world wars. In the book, the protagonist Hans Castorp leaves behind "the flatlands" to live in a sanatorium in Davos. The sanatorium is full of characters that together symbolize various groups in pre-war Europe. Mann's masterpiece is often cited as one of the most influential books of the 20th century. Like Castorp, I wanted to go far above the flatlands to gaze down at the world below. What has become of us humans? What does it mean to live in the early part of the 21st century? What are the ideas that shape us?

My eyes wander across the mountain range – now bathing in sunlight – and I ask these questions. The answer is silence.

Ironic.

Given that the flatlands are loud.

Very loud.

Louder than they have been for a century.

INTRODUCTION

WHERE DOES THE FUTURE COME FROM?

When my son was five, he suffered a seizure. We were in a car, he feel asleep and then seemed to wake up but was non-responsive and started grinding his teeth.

Me and my wife did not know what to make of it and so we buried our heads in the sand for about a year, having consulted Doctor Google who reassured us that it was probably nothing serious but mere sleepwalking, which seemed to make sense as my mother-in-law is known to walk in her sleep. What is parenthood if not a fine line between panic and denial?

He had four more seizures until we snapped out of our state of denial and took him to a doctor who diagnosed him with epilepsy. A magnetic brain scan revealed no damage or lesions to his brain that could explain the illness so we were left with a mystery. None of the medical staff we consulted knew what caused the seizures, or if the disease would go away with age.

Outside the medical profession, there was no lack of amateurs, zealots and "helpful" strangers offering their own theories – from self-proclaimed "gluten warriors" blaming all things wheat to poorly researched books blaming excessive iPad use. Conspiracies help people cope with the frustration of mystery.

I had always held the medical establishment as the very pinnacle of scientific knowledge in society – the shining light of enlightenment. This mystery – a black hole on the map – opened my eyes to a different world, or rather, a different view of our world.

The Dark Ages were never completely obliterated; we still live with mystery all around us.

A close family friend died from a particularly aggressive form of cancer. None of the experts knew what caused it or what to do about it.

In pharmaceutical research, of the drugs approved by the United States Federal Drug Administration in the first decade of this century, only a third came from target-based research. The rest came from discoveries made by chance, often by chemists who did not set out knowing what the drugs' targets were or how they worked.

If we zoom out from healthcare, and look at how famous innovations came about, mystery, chance and accident often play a significant part.

Drunk driving can generate a billion dollar business idea.

Playing around in a lab on a Friday afternoon can generate a Nobel Prize winning discovery.

Musical jamming can create a global smash hit, seemingly at random.

Poison can end up saving lives.

Failure can be the key to success, not its polar opposite.

Personal experimentation in the privacy of your kitchen can change the world.

These discoveries present a stark contrast to the kind of thinking about the future that we have grown accustomed to over the past decade. Politicians, pundits, entrepreneurs and thinkers have urged us to come up with large-scale, bold ideas to change the world. There is an abundant use of the word "big" to describe everything from computing to society: "Big Data", "Big Brother", "Big Society", "The Big Five" and so on. It seemed to make sense in this large, globalized world to talk about big ideas to solve big challenges like climate change and poverty. Surely, there could be nothing wrong if leaders prodded us to rise to the occasion.

Yet the stories of discovery I found were not about group efforts, polarizing battle cries or big ideas, they were personal moments, often involved failure and got results from doubt, uncertainty and experimentation.

A question formed itself in my head: Have we lost small ideas in the hunt for big ideas?

Have we lost useful insights from the pre-Enlightenment world – where mystery, alchemy and magic reigned supreme?

Is there a place for small ideas in the world of grand narratives?

The questions would not leave me alone.

The questions inspired this book.

Stockholm, February 2016

CHAPTER

1

BLANKET-BOMBED BY BLAH-BLAH

We live in times of danger and uncertainty. Of big ideas with great impact. We live in times where civilizations and religions are clashing. The fall of the west and the rise of the rest. We live in times of disruption where robots will steal our jobs and the middle class is automated into oblivion. We live in a time of global warming and heated debate. We live in times of inequality, of injustice with great potential consequences for the coming century, possibly the coming millennium.

We live in times of mass migration and displacement.

We live in times of big shifts and singularities.

We live in unprecedented times. The best of times or the worst of times? Who cares when they are unprecedented?

Most importantly, we live in times where a lot of people like to use these five words: "We live in times of… "

Objective reality is hidden behind a cacophony of voices growing ever louder in their attempts to drown each other out. Blogs, tweets, op-eds, talk shows, political speeches and YouTube videos scream at us that *this* particular idea is the one that deserves all the attention because of its stellar importance for humanity.

How did things get so loud and so furious?

Let us time-travel to the renowned TED (Technology, Entertainment, Design) conference in Monterrey, California back in February, 2006, so I can show you where I first noticed the increased focus on big ideas.

"Ideas Worth Spreading"

TED was for a long time a well-kept secret where a few hundred California geeks and entrepreneurs would meet and get inspired. The conference's creator, Richard Saul Wurman, had a vision of a panel- and podium-free informal conference built around quick talks aiming to inspire and enlighten. He sold the conference in the early 2000s to a British-born world citizen called Chris Anderson who took it from a 300-delegate conference in Monterrey to a global behemoth attended by thousands and watched by millions. When I started attending TED in 2005, this transformation was just about to get underway and the spirit was still that of a local event full of eclectic ideas and eccentric people. I fell in love with the conference. Being surrounded by so much intelligence and inspiration had a dazzling effect on me.

The spirit of the conference soon changed. Gone was the breezy, feather-light, Californian touch of my first TED where all kinds of ideas – big, small, strange and stupid – bounced around in a playful, gentle manner. At TED 2006, big, weighty themes awaited. Al Gore broke the 18-minute time limit and spoke for an hour about climate change – the same talk that would later win him an Academy Award and a Nobel Prize. A session entitled "A sharp intake of breath" would have been more suitably entitled "A sharp intake of death" as diseases, poverty and the annihilation of nature were discussed. Whereas TED 2005 had been a bottom-up event where you could make what you wanted out of the fragmented ideas presented, TED 2006 was firmly top-down and we were told to join in the march to save the planet.

This trend would grow stronger over the coming years as TED grew in stature and reach. When it opened its video library to the world, it made superstars of keynote speakers and the most watched videos generated hundreds of millions of views. They launched a prize to reward the world's best and most impactful thinkers. They hammered in the slogan "Ideas Worth Spreading" whenever and wherever they could. Furthermore, TED set a global agenda in which the "save the world"-mantra spread to everything from TV commercials for banks to pop star tweets.

In 2013, I discovered the transformation of TED from bottom-up eccentricity to top-down opinion-former had a very particular cause.

I was invited to speak at a conference hosted by a well-known financial-services company. Before the main program began, VIP delegates had a chance to book one-on-one sessions with the speakers. The Chinese professor had dozens of sessions booked. The ex-President had too many to handle. I had one session booked. I sat in a small meeting room with no window and was introduced to Mike Novogratz. Since my knowledge of the financial world was and still is somewhat limited, I really had no idea who he was. Bald-headed, friendly, informal with great wit and intelligence, we had a lovely chat. It was only later that I found out that he is a billionaire in charge of one of the world's most famous hedge funds, Fortress. The reason he had booked a one-on-one with me was that I had described myself as a TED attendee in the speaker biography.

As I told him about the transformation of TED, he laughed and said jokingly: "Yeah, my sister kind of ruined it." It turned out that his sister is Jacqueline Novogratz who had met and married TED curator Chris Anderson around that same time. Jacqueline Novogratz is an activist and entrepreneur whose investment company, Acumen Fund, was built to address global poverty. She is passionate about aid, entrepreneurship, African development and many other topics that made their presence felt at TED 2006. One could say that Jacqueline Novogratz took TED's slogan from "ideas worth spreading" to "big, important ideas worth spreading a lot more than just any random idea."

The Big Idea Future

The future is a story more than it is a place on the timeline. When we begin sentences with the words "in the future", we are telling a story about a time and place where things will be different from today. As a story, the future has four archetypes: Progress, Decline, Cyclicality and Discontinuity. Progress is the idea that things are, in general, getting better. Decline takes the opposite view and argues that things are, in general, getting worse. Cyclicality sits firmly in the middle and argues that history repeats itself in an infinite loop whilst discontinuity takes the viewpoint that rules are always rewritten and the past, as well as the future, are foreign lands, even alien planets to our familiar present. These four themes can be seen in future thinking historically ranging from the optimism of the post-World War II years in Europe to the kind of pessimism characterizing debates about climate change today. What is peculiar about the 2010's is that these four different stories can coexist and their followers radicalized. Here's how each archetype is presented in this "Decade of Big Ideas":

- **Progress**
  The world is growing infinitely richer and healthier. No mystery is too difficult for the world to solve. Whether it is curing a previously fatal disease or putting a woman on Mars, we can do it. The idea of progress is fairly new in the history of mankind. For thousands of years, we could not make prosperity – only take it from others. The idea of progress is, in other words, sympathetic

The Four Archetypes of Future Stories

PROGRESS
is the idea
that things are,
in general
getting better.

DECLINE
takes the opposite
view and argues
that things are,
in general,
getting worse.

FUTURE

CYCLICALITY
sits firmly in
the middle and
argues that history
repeats itself in an
infinite loop.

DISCONTINUITY
takes the viewpoint that
rules are always rewritten
and the past, as well as
the future, are foreign
lands, even alien planets
to our familiar present.

and optimistic. Until it gets challenged by rampant pessimism, however, and needs to scream at the top of its lungs that the world is growing infinitely better, all the time, in every possible direction. Not so much "seeing is believing" as "believing is seeing." It has become somewhat fashionable to be an optimist, especially if you are a techno-utopian, where you carry – and broadcast – a firm belief in the rejuvenating powers of capitalism and technology. This was illustrated by one of the characters in the TV show *Silicon Valley*, a comedy focused on Californian technology entrepreneurs: "I don't want to live in a world where somebody else makes the world a better place than we do."

"We humans have never been healthier and wealthier than we are today", "The future is bright and abundant – what is scarce today will be in excess tomorrow", "Technology will free us all", "The poorest person today is richer than the rich were a hundred years ago", "We have eradicated illness/ hunger/poverty."

● Decline

Ominous clouds gather on the horizon – from climate change and multi-resistant bacteria to barbarians at the gate and looming wars. The past decade has been particularly favourable to pessimists with many armchair futurists proclaiming the fall of the EU, of the West, of the economy and of capitalism itself. The threats, we are told, are greater than they have ever been. Now is the time to act if we want to avoid Armageddon. Actually, others add, it is already too late and we must face a future of adapting to living with Armageddon. Technology, used by the progressive side as a force for good, here becomes the father of a master race that will enslave us all with seductive social media apps and make us jobless through work-stealing robots. Like devout believers, we are told that we should repent, or should that be "disrupt"?

"We are entering an age of uncertainty, fear and volatility", "We are facing the biggest challenges mankind has ever faced", "A comet/climate change/epidemic threatens our very existence", "We will remember the past as a time of great stability and tranquillity", "Change your ways ... or else!"

● **Cyclicality**

"History is a wheel, for the nature of man is fundamentally unchanging. What has happened before will perforce happen again." The words come from one of the most popular TV shows in the world – *Game of Thrones*. Although it is set in a medieval world with dragons, its themes resonate with 21st century audiences since it reflects what they see when they look at the modern world. Economists point to the 1970s; historians to the 1910-1920 period; technologists to the 1890s. And religious zealots point to the descriptions of ancient words in holy books. We only need to look behind us to go forward since everything that has been will be again. Progress and decline are similar since they involve momentum, albeit in different directions. The cyclical world, however, is truly hopeless since mankind remains stuck on the treadmill of eternity. Like Sisyphus rolling his rock or Wile E Coyote chasing that damn bird, there is no destination or resolution in sight.

"Our decade is just like the 1970s/ 1930s/ 1890s."

● **Discontinuity**
Everything we know will change. Call it The Singularity* or The Rapture**, the ideas is that all rules, and reality itself, will change over night. This is similar to the idea of a coming Armageddon with the intention to defuse present ideas about the future by arguing that they will

be obsolete in the coming "New Normal". What good is a carbon tax if we are heading towards The Rapture? What is the point of selling beer if we are heading towards the Singularity? The present is seen as an inflection point and a portal into a future so radically different from now as to be unrecognisable. It is rhetorically hard to argue with proponents of this archetype. If Everything will be different, the old rules, existing knowledge and current arguments will not apply. It is eerily similar to the way religious fanatics defend their faith by saying that mere human words or thoughts can never fathom divine greatness. Author and thinker Jaron Lanier describes it as follows: "[Discontinuity] is really about religion, people turning to metaphysics to cope with the human condition. They have a way of dramatizing their beliefs with an end-of-days scenario – and one does not want to criticize other people's religions."

> "The old rules will no longer apply",
> "Everything we know is wrong",
> "Artificial intelligence/the rise of China/rising sea levels will change everything."

*   The Singularity: a popular idea in future thinking describing a hypothetical moment in time when artificial intelligence will have progressed to the point of a greater-than-human intelligence.

** The Rapture: A Christian end of time event when all true believers who are still alive will be taken from the earth by God into heaven.

29

Monsters In The Closet

These four archetypes of future thinking have been transformed from forecasts to fearcasts intended to threaten, subdue and polarize debates with a "with us or against us"– rhetoric. Followers of each camp see themselves as the enlightened minority whose mission is to guide the rest of us into a catharsis that will cleanse us, transform us and make us believe in the one true path. If we can all just emit less carbon dioxide or invest more money or get used to living without economic growth or rewrite all the rules, eternal happiness would be ours. Historians talk about the "Great Man theory," the idea that significant events in history were created by great, heroic individuals. What we see today is a kind of "Great Vision theory" where the most compelling, grand narrative that attracts the most followers will change history's arrow.

The most frightening horror movies are the ones where the ghosts and ghouls remain off-screen. Childhood is defined by insecurity about what we cannot see – might there be monsters in the closet or under the bed? It seems like this fear is now following us into adulthood, as perfectly rational grownups will speak of the future as if it contains some unimaginable beast ready to devour us all, whether it is robots replacing humans, rising sea levels making Earth uninhabitable or a previously peaceful state turning belligerent and triggering a world war.

Progressivists, Declinists, Cyclicists and Discontinuit-ists use similar tactics of persuasion to bring their point across. They offer redemption through agreement and threaten rejection through disagreement. If you don't see how robots will change everything or that the atmospheric carbon dioxide level is society's most pressing need, there simply is no hope for you. You may even be branded a "luddite" or "denier". They also rely on eschatological elements – the idea that the world is about to end. Even Progressivists, optimistic by nature, talk about The Singularity – the point in time where technology becomes the dominant life force and liberates us humans. The pattern emerging is that the archetypical stories have moved from factual observations to religious scripture. The world may have grown more secular in the past century but a collective spiritual yearning has manifested itself in the stories we tell about the future.

This leaves two important questions to be answered: why did we come to this and why does it matter? The next chapter will try to answer both questions.

CHAPTER

WELCOME TO THE SECEITY

The underpinning idea of a society is to strive towards common goals and traits – to create a "we". Lately, we can see the emergence of The Seceity – a hybrid of the words secession and society – wherein the idea is to gravitate towards differences – in class, skin colour, gender, background and experience. Identity and ideology have coalesced to a point where simply saying someone is a "white, heterosexual, middle-class male" is to label him with opinions. That he might not necessarily share these opinions or, more importantly, that he wants to be seen as an individual, not a slave to his skin or gender, is beside the point. In The Seceity, everyone is a part of a group whether they want to be or not and the pecking order is designed to reverse the injustice of times gone by. Hence, the opinion of a privileged white, middle-class person is of limited interest and impact whereas the opinion of a coloured, transgender person from a poor background is seen as wiser, richer and of greater significance. In The Seceity, you fit in by standing out and special character traits – no matter how lucky or unlucky you are to have gotten them – call for special benefits. This, understandably, angers a lot of people but in their haste to condemn The Seceity, they lash out at superficial manifestations of it, not its root causes. They will blame the media climate in general and social media in particular. They will blame whichever group stands the furthest from their own opinions. They will complain about "political correctness" or a general lack of political leadership. And so on. The reality is that these superficial, sloppily argued yet emotionally charged accusations only make them a cog in The Seceity's machine – yet another group of people calling foul. What really caused The Seceity to emerge runs deeper and paints a more interesting portrait of our modern world.

Something Happened on the Way to Paradise

I was born in Sweden in the 1970s so my adolescence was marked by a continuous series of endings – from the fall of communism to the end of the Cold War. It seemed like all the talk about world peace was working. For Americans and Europeans, it was like conflict, war and poverty were historical relics along with high oil prices and state-owned monopolies. When conflicts came knocking on our door yet again in the 2000s, I was shocked, saddened and bewildered. I was not alone in this feeling with *TIME* magazine branding the first ten years of the millennium "The decade from hell."

What was it that turned the world on its head ?

The common answers involved Al Qaeda, China, commodities, financial markets and the internet. Although these factors explain volatility and danger, they do not necessarily explain the intellectual battles that characterize The Seceity. To understand why the world became a shout-fest of grand narratives, we need to analyse how information and its nature had changed. Like a drunk driver, information flows changed direction drastically and erratically in the late 1990s. The flows had for centuries followed a hierarchical path, flowing from the leaders on top of the pyramid down to the followers on the lower echelons. All of a sudden, this path was reversed, and dispersed. Information started flowing from anyone to everyone and back again. This had several knock-on effects:

- **Information became a buffet:** From making do with the morning newspaper and the evening news on TV, we were offered news in all kinds of formats and channels. And not just news – porn, games, gossip, music and anything we could think of. In unlimited supply. WWW was not only an acronym for the World Wide Web but increasingly came to mean whatever, whenever and wherever. In this "buffetisation" of information, we started seeking out what we liked and preferred, not what the chef or rations subjected us to. It also meant that The Truth – previously a monolithic concept – became My Truth – a more subjective and deceptive concept.

- **Everyone suddenly knew everything:** Information used to be power and those who had it would rule over us who did not. Suddenly, everyone knew everything, whether it was how to solve the Middle Eastern conflict or who really caused the financial crisis of 2008. Conviction replaced curiosity and listening turned into shouting.

- **The Moon-walking ratio increased:** This ratio describes the difference between second-hand information – things you have seen on TV or read about – and first-hand information – things you have actually experienced. The reason everyone suddenly knew everything was not because they had begun to travel more extensively, but because the accessibility of other people's accounts, photos and opinions increased. It is called The Moon-walking ratio because everyone knows what the surface of the moon looks like and what it is like to walk on it, yet only 12 people have ever done it.

- **The Post-Fact Society:** Speaking of moon-walking, there is infinite evidence that the moon landings never happened. Just like there is infinite evidence that God exists and that airplanes leave behind chemical trails or "chemtrails" to subdue humans and hide some kind of mysterious planet. When we are left to our own devices about what to believe, many will choose to believe anything – especially if it makes the world easier to understand or more exciting to live in. President John F. Kennedy put it as follows: "The great enemy of truth is very often not the lie – deliberate, contrived and dishonest – but the myth – persistent, persuasive and unrealistic."

- **The rise of charismatic power:** The political philosopher Max Weber divided power into three categories: traditional, rational and charismatic. Traditional power is the kind that is inherited and passed on through generations, in the way of royal families. Rational power is what somebody gains when he presents a better solution to current problems. The final category is especially pronounced across the world today: charismatic power. In this category, the actual ideas and their usefulness of a person matter less than his appearance – the way he looks, sounds and the way he presents his ideas. This kind of power is especially seductive if the problems we face are complex and require difficult, long-winded solutions. Refugees, climate change, war, technological developments, unemployment and macroeconomics all fit that description so it is no wonder that electorates from east to west choose a fun, easy to understand populist when they go to the polls.

- **Information Ghettoes:** Imagine the velvet rope of an exclusive nightclub. All you need to get that friendly wave from the bouncer and enter is the right opinions. This is what abundant access to information has created – a world of silos and ghettoes where your opinions and how you personify them are what connects you to other people. If information is cheap and ubiquitous, perspectives – *how* you see information – matter more than the information content itself. Furthermore, we can easily connect with strangers around the world especially if we are interested in the same things, be it conspiracy theories or cats resembling Josef Stalin. These ghettoes of the like-minded exist not only for the narrow-minded. Extensive specialization in the professional field has also contributed. Imagine a sandbox in a playground where children come to have fun. Anyone can dig a hole and play in a sandbox. However, if we keep digging down to, say, two or three meters, play becomes hobby – a pit you keep digging in for a few hours every day after school or work. Dig even further, down tens or hundreds of meters, and hobby becomes profession with equipment, budgets and project planning. It is now dangerous for children to come near the sandbox. Finally, if we dig deep enough, we consult scientific research to understand the consequences of digging near the earth's core so there are only a handful of experts in the world who have the knowledge we need. The welcoming, inclusive atmosphere of the playground has become an isolated field – a silo – of scientific inquiry cordoned off from the rest of society. You don't need to dig a mine to create The Seceity. All you need are the following words: "You don't understand me because you don't have access to my perspective." In The Seceity, we strive for differences, not commonalities.

Babble-On Babylon

Having established why we are blanket-bombed by blah-blah, we must try to answer the question "So what?" Why does this matter? In a free society, people are entitled to believe in and talk about whatever they want, right? Absolutely. The purpose of this book is not to share opinions about other people's opinions – there is enough of that in The Seceity already. Neither is this book a nostalgic lament for simpler times gone by that pins the blame on social media or excessive globalization. *Minifesto* is an inquiry into the role of ideas in creating the future. These first two chapters have sought to describe a world in which grand narratives – really big ideas – battle to shape our views of the future using divisive language and scare tactics. The interesting question is not necessarily whether these narratives will turn out to be correct but what we lose when we impose top-down, with-us-or-against-us stories onto ourselves, our friends, our colleagues and our children.

What happens when we let feelings – not thoughts or rational argument – become the main currency in debates? The psychologist Carl Jung argued that thinking is difficult, so most people merely judge.

What happens when we do not hear whispering opportunities because a chorus of screaming problems drowns them out?

What happens when we evaluate scenarios not by their actual plausibility but by the way they are presented, and awestruck becomes dumbstruck?

It is tempting to let these questions hover, but we do know a couple of things about what happens, ranging from the superficial to the profound.

Firstly – and most trivially – the opportunity cost of focusing heavily on only one scenario can be very high. An example is the irrational exuberance in the dot-com boom of the late 1990s where investors everywhere praised and poured money into the stocks of online companies. Many failed yet a minority – like Amazon and Ebay – went on to earn hundreds of percentage points in returns over the coming decade, which may sound impressive. It pales in comparison, however, when we look at energy drinks, at the time overshadowed and overlooked. The share price of Monster Drinks – one of the bigger manufacturers – has risen 53.000% between March 2000 and 2015. By myopically zooming in on one idea or industry, opportunities in other sectors are ignored.

Secondly, grouping ideas into "isms" simplifies thinking and obscures objectivity. Take the common optimism/pessimism-lens as an example. On the whole, people are far too optimistic and judge their own abilities too highly – a cognitive bias known in psychology as "illusory superiority" – while they misjudge common risks with a shrug and "it won't happen to me" mindset. Pessimism is a survival skill, but it skews our view of reality. Take the supposedly unsinkable ship that sailed from South-ampton to New York in the early 1910s. Most people will associate that description with the infamous RMS Titanic yet its identical sister ship RMS Olympic made that jour-ney many times between 1911 and its retirement in 1935. No movies are made about sailing through storms and icebergs and arriving safely. Similarly, we all know what happens to rock stars and movie stars when they turn 27, right? Most people point to the so-called "27 Club", a claim that celebrities have a tendency to die or commit suicide at that age, like Janis Joplin and Kurt Cobain. In reality, many artists produce their finest, most successful work at that age – from U2's The Joshua Tree, Bjork's Debut and Radiohead's The Bends to Steve Jobs starting work on the game changing Apple Macintosh computer and William Shakespeare making his debut. By clinging on to a heuris-tic – "the world is good" or "the world is bad" – we often miss the real, and more interesting, stories.

Thirdly, progress – in biology and economy – requires variation. Variety is not just a spice of life but one of its fundamental building blocks. Adaptation in nature hap-pens not because individual species quickly change to meet new conditions, but because of variety in the spe-cies themselves. Some birds are born with long beaks, some with short. Some plants require a lot of sunlight to grow, some only a tiny bit. The future is not a chess game of black versus white but a giant roulette table where you place your bets on many different squares and colours.

A lack of variety is damaging. Mono-cultural agriculture – focusing on growing only one crop, like corn, over many years – depletes the earth and leaves the ecosystem vulnerable. Similarly, a town with only one big employer has a tendency to fade away when the employer goes belly-up. Detroit and its dependency on the US automotive industry is an example. Cities – vibrant, diverse, and full of employment opportunities big and small – never disappear, but grow rapidly as they attract people fleeing poverty in the countryside or the lack of opportunity in smaller towns. For companies, variety – or innovation as it is more popularly called – ensures longevity. Communism failed not because its basic principle – equality for all – is bad, but because the regimes that implemented communism were forced to come up with new ideas for every five-year plan. This works as long as the imagination of the rulers exceeds that of the population but over time, the system went bankrupt – first from a lack of ideas, then from a lack of money. Wandering through any supermarket is testament to the ingenuity and variety of humans – from cherry-flavoured toothpicks to triple-quilted extra soft toilet paper. Capitalism is arguably more chaotic than communism but that is its main strength, not its fatal flaw.

Grand narratives lower variety in an economy, distort our view of reality and force us to make the wrong decisions – about where to invest and what to do in life. Furthermore, when we loudly proclaim, with great certainty, that the future is about exactly this or exactly that, we craft a kind of thought prison wherein any conversation about the future must use the future scenario as its base line – be it climate change, technology, globalization or gender equality. There is no place for silliness like fashion, popular culture or meaningless ideas in the thought prison of a big, important idea. The irony is that the modern economy runs not on *one* big idea but on burgers, blue jeans, computer games, electric toasters and plastic Christmas trees. It runs on variety in people. An economy with only 20 very rich people would be a very poor economy. An economy selling only basic necessities would quickly exhaust its resources. What we fail to see when we nod in agreement with big, important thinkers and frown at a frivolous supermarket aisle is that the modern economy is a transformational reallocation mechanism, wherein a dental floss purchase can pay for healthcare, a smart phone purchase can pay for cancer research and a pair of slim-fit jeans can feed a family. For this system to thrive, we need experimentation, doubt, contradiction and an even greater variety of stories about the future.

Prelude to The Minifesto

We should not become slaves to other people's opinions about the future. That is the simple reason this book exists. Creativity should not be taken hostage by proponents of big ideas when it needs freedom to breathe – freedom to be, think and do. "Freedom from …" before "freedom to …".

The "we" of the future has been torn apart by an us-and-them mentality used to strengthen the grand narratives – are you a climate supporter or a climate-change denier? Are you unfairly rich or unfairly poor? Are you a technophile or a Luddite? Are you a native or an immigrant? It is no coincidence that William Butler Yeats's poem *The Second Coming* is so often quoted these days with its foreboding lines: "The best lack all conviction, while the worst are full of passionate intensity."

Passionate intensity – so seductive and so bewildering. The Minifesto wants to explore what happens when we explore the opposite – mild curiosity, doubt, scepticism, disillusion, nothingness – and how it can lead to even greater miracles. For ourselves, for the economy and for the future.

Let us leave The Seceity behind us.

Imagine the noise slowly fading as we slowly rise to higher ground.

The voices, tweets, op-eds and headlines become blurry, then silent, then invisible.

We go through the clouds.

We fly past The Magic Mountain.

To land somewhere unexpected.

CHAPTER

THE MOMENT OF CREATION

We are in the passenger seat of a car travelling through Florida in the 1950s. Sitting behind the wheel is James McLamore, a small business owner from Miami. The ride is probably noisy because of the cranky quality of cars back then. What's worse is that McLamore – Jim to his friends – is getting drunk on bourbon and Dr Pepper whilst driving.

CUT TO

We are sitting on a porch in the Swedish countryside in the 1970s. It's midsummer and the sun is already up, although it's still the early hours, say around 3 a.m. With us are Carl-Jan Granqvist, a young chef who would decades later become a celebrity in Sweden, Sven Trägårdh, a wine importer and Jens Spendrup, a down-on-his-luck beer brewer. It is the aftermath of a birthday celebration for a mutual friend and these are the last men standing – or, more accurately, sitting.

CUT TO

We are in a recording studio in New York City in the early 2000s. Behind the microphone in the singing booth is Amy Winehouse, a young jazz singer. She has just spent some time talking to the producer Mick Ronson about her tempestuous relationship with her boyfriend. The relationship serves as a basis for the songs she is about to record. Roll tape.

CUT TO

A woman is taking a smoking break at Sahlgrenska Hospital in Gothenburg, Sweden and far away from her, in Australia, a large agrochemical company is excited about a new kind of herbicide that would later prove a disaster.

CUT TO

An elbow knocking over a torsion spring.

CUT TO

A woman having a dream.

CUT TO

A guy drunk in a bar.

Meet The Alchemists of Creation

These situations are the introduction scenes to some truly remarkable ideas, works of art, innovations and business concepts but they look like meaningless moments in the steady stream of random events we call life. Yet the stillness is deceiving. In the words of musician Peter Gabriel: "Sometimes, when you look around, everything seems still and calm on the surface, and then you detect a little disturbance, and you know for sure, that underneath the surface lies some other secret world." This secret, invisible world is the great muse of many artists. Tom Stoppard has the following famous passage in his play Arcadia: "The ordinary-sized stuff which is our lives, the things people write poetry about – clouds – daffodils – waterfalls – and what happens in a cup of coffee when the cream goes in – these things are full of mystery, as mysterious to us as the heavens were to the Greeks." Norwegian novelist Karl Ove Knausgård says that the ordinary, everyday life is full of invisible things that are dramatic. Knausgård, in turn, is often referred to as the "alchemist of the ordinary". The choice of metaphor is interesting because alchemy is often used to describe something esoteric, abstract and spiritual. The alchemists, hobby scientists that preceded The Enlightenment, were in a quest to understand the world of materials and, most infamously, turn lead into gold. What separated alchemists from scientists was the isolated nature of their work where individuals worked hard to keep their goals and results private as opposed to publishing them in a scientific journal for anyone to read and scrutinize. The reason for the secrecy of alchemists is as simple as it is misguided – turning lead into a precious metal is only valuable if nobody else can do it, otherwise gold is commoditised and becomes as worthless as lead. Alchemy transformed into science when the practitioners started sharing their results. The modern concept of innovation – finding new ideas – is more like alchemy than it is like science. Companies design their own processes to hunt for new devices, models and ways of doing things and then guard them fiendishly – through patents and confidentiality clauses – since the "new, new thing" is only a competitive advantage if nobody else has access to it. This is why there is no recipe for innovation because if there was, everyone would do exactly the same thing and innovation would lose its significance as a means to build a fortune. Alchemy will serve as our starting point when we study how ideas emerge.

Phlogiston Moments

Alchemists famously divided the world into four elements: earth, wind, water and fire. There was also a mysterious fifth element called *phlogiston*. The belief was that phlogiston was a fiery combustible material embedded in other bodies. If something burnt with extra intensity, like magnesium, it was rich in phlogiston. This was before the discovery of oxygen – the invisible element enabling oxidization – so one can see why the misunderstanding happened.

When a person has a new idea – seemingly out of nowhere – it is a phlogiston moment. Something catches fire within you – you see things clearly, you see its potential, something fits, the puzzle is complete. We don't know why it happens – we might discover something akin to oxidization within our consciousness in some far-off century using new scientific methods and measurement tools

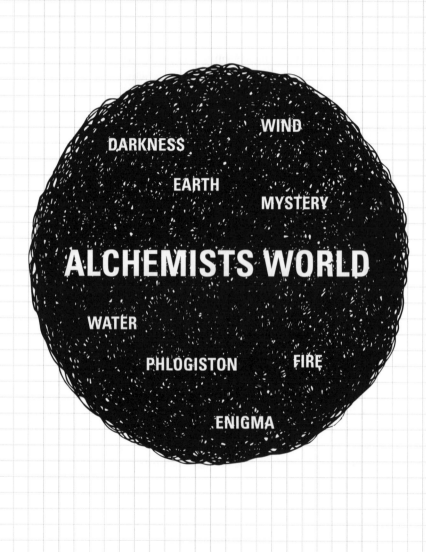

– but we all know the feeling of a phlogiston moment. McLamore, drunk driver. Spendrup, the brewer. The smoking woman. Winehouse, the jazz singer. And the many other examples to be explored in the coming chapters are all examples of the power of phlogiston moments. In the grand narrative-view of the world, the connection between inspiration, idea and outcome are linear and causal: "If we state that problem x is important enough to solve, a bunch of innovators will come up with a solution that will solve problem x." The underlying belief of phlogiston moments is that few – if any – things function in such a simplistic manner. Reality is characterized by its lack of straightforwardness, by its indirect causes, by luck and serendipity. In short, life is characterized by its obliquity, to use a wonderfully obscure and mysterious word.

SOLUTION

PROBLEM

CUT TO

Frank Sinatra, lost and forgotten, singing in a small town in Sweden in 1953 with only a handful of people in the audience.

CUT TO

Ray Wagner, working for a toy manufacturer, turning down the license to make Star Wars toys in the 1970s.

CUT TO

A young Italian man turning a salad bowl upside down to invent the modern kitchen lamp.

CHAPTER

4

THE DIFFERENCE BETWEEN IDEAS AND IDEAS

We have one word – idea – to describe a complex bundle of insights, neural network activity, synapses and narratives. Yet, like the supposedly verbally gifted Eskimos describing snow, we would need hundreds of terms to distinguish between the kind of Eureka-moments that hit you in the shower and the accidental insights you gain from misunderstanding something. For the sake of simplicity, we shall divide the world of ideas into two spheres: pet ideas and wild ideas. Pet ideas are tame, cuddly, docile and live in symbiosis with humans. Wild ideas are, well, wild, unpredictable, roam free and seemingly have a life of their own. Here are sets of words that can be associated with each sphere.

The World of Ideas
– Pet Ideas and Wild Ideas

PET IDEAS

- Compete
- Fit In
- Sunflowers
- Big Ideas
- The Future
- Travel to Arrive
- Origin Matters
- The World Is Flat
- Good Ideas
- Creationism
- Knowing
- Recipes
- Certainty
- Insurance
- Should

WILD IDEAS

- Create
- Break In
- Bougainvillea
- Small Ideas
- To Future
- Travel to Get Lost
- Origin Does Not Matter
- The World is a Mountain
- Bad Ideas
- Darwinism
- Not Knowing
- Sparks
- Doubt
- Discovery
- Could

Compete or Create?

We can choose between two paths in how we work, live and thrive. We can choose to compete – from the Latin *com petare*, strive together – a social exercise wherein we compare ourselves to others and try to fit in and excel. Winning is awesome. In sports you get a medal when you win. In business, winning is associated with bumper profits and champagne. The feedback loop for competition is rather pleasant – we get to race, excel and win.

The other path is to create, a much less comfortable endeavour. The reason is that we tend to be sceptical when somebody creates something new – be it a work of art, a new technology, a new medical practice – and say things like "it won't work" or "you must be mad." If the initial scepticism is overcome and the idea gains some popularity, it will polarize people. Some will love you – for being brave and doing new things – whereas others will hate you, oppose you, ridicule you, maybe even try to kill you. Creation is a lonely path, full of obstacles and often without a clear goal. We have two paths to choose from – compete or create – but one of them seduces far more people with its promises of champagne, popularity and strive-togetherness.

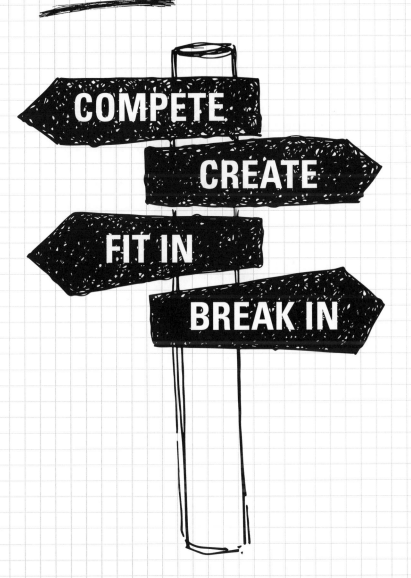

Fit in or Break in?

Fitting in is about adapting – speak like others speak, dress like they dress, respect the codes and adapt to the culture. It does not matter if you are a Swede trying to fit in Switzerland or a Sudanese trying to fit in Sweden, the rules are the same: listen, learn, follow. Breaking in is the opposite. Here, you stay unique and make a big noise as you announce your entrance. You keep your quirks, your asymmetries and your irritable traits. The world of soft drinks was dominated by the Cokes and Pepsis of the world until Red Bull broke in. The world of rock music was dominated by big hair bands and pretty boys until Nirvana broke in. The world of movies was about glamour, gloss and big budgets until the Danish Dogma movement broke in.

Sunflowers or Bougainvillea?

Some ideas are like sunflowers – beautiful to look at, easy to understand and you can even cut them off, bring them home and they will stay beautiful even when they have dried up. Other ideas are like bougainvillea, a messy jumble of vines and leaves. There is no beginning or end and you certainly cannot cut a part off to convey its beauty – it will look like dead leaves.

Sunflower ideas are the kind that we like to share, blog about and loudly proclaim "this exact idea is the future."

Bougainvillea ideas are like networks and cannot be pin-pointed, nailed down or even articulated. They just kind of exist without anyone stopping to admire their peculiar beauty or inherent life force.

Big or Small?

Is it better to take one giant leap or a thousand small steps?

Big ideas seek consensus: "Yes, this is big!" the crowds say in unison. To be big, they must be understood by many and therefore cannot be too complex. To be big, they must address problems shared by many and to be shared by many, it must be dramatic and worthy of big news headlines. Big ideas should sound like they could instantly solve these big, pressing problems. When a big idea fails, it affects many.

Small ideas do not need consensus. They do not need the voice of the many or their understanding. They can be weird, dumb, abstract, peculiar or just very hard to understand no matter how high your IQ is. When a small idea fails, nothing happens. In the big-idea world, a book about love is called "Behold The Awesome Power of Love." In the small-idea world, the book about love is called *Anna Karenina* or *Wuthering Heights*.

The Future or To Future?

The Future is a noun, a place, and if we climb high enough or buy expensive measuring tools, we will be able to see The Future before anyone else.

To Future is a verb, an activity, that describes the constant grappling with decisions, the failed plans, the broken promises and the dense fog that forever surrounds that mystical word "tomorrow".

Travel to Arrive or Travel to Get Lost?

Travel is a hassle to many people – from the busy morning commute to the security check before a long-haul flight. Travelphobics – the official term is *hodophobia*, an irrational fear of travel – like these will dream about teleportation machines and flying cars to cut away the time spent getting from A to B.

The other kind of traveller loves getting lost – finding oneself in an unexpected part of Buenos Aires, a dead-end street in London or some remote part of Burma. Ubiquitous GPS-enabled mobile phones have made this kind of traveller a near-extinct species.

Origin Matters or Origin Does Not Matter?

We live in a world where "Who" or "By Whom?" is not just nice-to-know but need-to-know for many people. They believe that what someone – artist, inventor, creator – has made cannot be disentangled from who they are. Therefore, superficial traits like skin colour and gender are treated like significant building blocks, not as the genetic accidents they are. The opposite view is to disregard who made it. It does not matter if the creator of a lifesaving vaccine believed in UFOs. It does not matter if the artist who brought joy to millions was a closet racist. It does not matter if the inventor of a great invention had bad breath and a rude manner.

Is the World flat or a Mountain?

Many believe that the world is a level playing field with emerging and emerged nations competing for resources, jobs and prosperity. The flat-world hypothesis permeates debates about salaries (they need to be competitive), school grades (the need to be in the global top 10 in standardized testing) and architecture (we should be as brave as Dubai or Shanghai when we build our cities). If, on the other hand, the world is a mountain, there are many things we have yet to explore – from the depths of the ocean and unknown plants of the jungle to secret dimensions in physics and unseen materials on other planets. In this world, the world is not a sports tournament but a journey of discovery. If the world is flat, we have to take. If the world is a mountain, we can make.

Good Ideas or Bad Ideas?

Good ideas are ideas that make people go "yes!" and "great!" or even "brilliant!" They are the kind of ideas that politicians talk about and conference delegates rave about. Good ideas are seen as important and the people that have them are invited to fancy dinners with important people. They get to be on the cover of magazines and they win prizes. Good ideas make us like ourselves even more. Bad ideas, meanwhile, are ugly and smell bad. They make people angry and leave the room. They are "boring!" or "ridiculous!" or just downright "stupid!" Bad ideas have no friends.

Creationism or Darwinism?

In Creationism, He made the world. He had a master plan – a vision – and then meticulously placed everything in its right place with focused intent and discipline. In this top-down view of the world, cities are built from scratch like in the computer game Sim City, companies are dictatorships built by a single-minded visionary and language, culture and nations are fortresses that need to be guarded from intruders intending to wreck them. In Darwinism, there is no He, no plan, no vision or intent. There is only randomness across oceans of time. There is no history, only one damn thing after another. There is no path or goal, only a wild river and adventures.

Knowing or Not Knowing?

Knowing stuff helps you get good grades and win board games like Trivial Pursuit. Knowing gets you a degree, a job and a salary. Knowing makes you interesting. Not knowing makes you interested. You will get no job, no salary and no quiz show prizes but you will have a chance to see the world anew. Every day.

Recipes or Sparks?

Recipes are one-way blueprints: Add x to y, wait and voilà! Recipes have by definition already been tried before and are passed on – like wisdom – through generations. They are a way to repeat the past over and over albeit with some improvisation, with a new ingredient every now and then. Sparks, on the other hand, just fly. They are the flaming residue from things colliding and tend to just vanish unless they accidentally ignite something. Before the invention of fire came the invention of sparks and they must have seemed like meaningless little fire-flies that would not amount to much. Most sparks are wasted but a few of them trigger something big.

Certainty or Doubt?

Certainty is bliss. I want this! I am sure of something! I know it to be true! Convictions are buoyant and save us from drowning. Certainty eliminates the anxiety caused by life's infinite choices. It clarifies, radiates and inspires. Doubt is a cold feeling of nothingness. I am nothing. It opens up vast worlds but leaves us no map so we are left with fears of getting trapped, lost, killed and eaten. Doubt is a leap of faith whereas certainty is faith leaping at you to hold you in its warm embrace.

Insurance or Discovery?

My father saw higher education as an insurance product. "It's always a good idea to go to university," he would say, "you never know what you want to do and where you will end up." At university, many students had the same kind of keep-as-many-doors-open mindset and never really committed to any singular vision, but instead studied broad, useful subjects like business administration and then went to work for management consultancies. Parents around the world seem to worry about the quality of schools today: "What will become of our children if they don't learn enough math or English?" As if education is an insurance against an unexpected future. The opposite of insurance is discovery – where you let the world take you wherever it wants and you adapt to the situation you will find yourself in. If we saw education as discovery, we would say things like "let's just see what happens" and "let's teach our children that nearly everything we know and have ever known is wrong."

Should or Could?

"We should do X" is completely different from "We could do X!" The former is leading, directional, intentional and possibly coercive. The latter is inclusive, experimental and inquisitive.

What we *should* do are things we can envision, articulate and project. What we *could* do are things we are unsure of, want to explore and understand. *Should* is inside-out whereas *could* is outside-in. *Should* is a charismatic leader in a shining armour. *Could* is a nerd with braces.

What Sphere Are You?

Books about pet ideas will be located in the Business Strategy or Self-Improvement sections of bookstores. They will feature heroic case studies about insnovative companies and inspiring individuals. They will give you checklists and recipes for how to become a hero yourself. They will be unambiguous, sharp and intelligent. Like a president or king.

Books about Wild Ideas don't exist because the ideas are difficult to pin down, study and share. Perhaps the fiction section of the bookstore will feature a few books about some inner journey, but the best thing you can do is to leave the bookstore and go out into the real world to where the wild things are.

Into The Wild

Ideas are rarely studied in their natural habitat. Like skeletons and fossils at the Natural History Museum, we usually see them much later when they have been used, abused, stripped of their original beauty and have clear names identifying their causes, uses and benefits. We never really get to feel the thrill of Leonardo Da Vinci scribbling something down. When we hear about his ideas, they have been repackaged like logical steps in a narrative that would always end up with Mona Lisa in the Louvre instead of the tinkering moments – the flying sparks – they once were.

What Manifestos Want

The Cathédrale Notre-Dame de Reims in France is a monumental building. To stand at its entrance and gaze upwards on the hundred meters tall, gothic façade is simply breathtaking. Built in the 13th century, it is a marriage of grand architecture and religion, which in this time before The Reformation and The Enlightenment was the binding glue and guiding hand in France and beyond. What is striking about the building – apart from its beauty and craftsmanship – is its size in relation to us humans standing at its doors. The cathedral is enormous while people are very, very small. This was the power ratio between religion and individuals for a very long time in human history: humans – small, expendable and insignificant; religion – universal, eternal and all-encompassing. The grand narratives of The Seceity are designed using a similar ratio. The future is seen as a large project that we should all yield to and bow in front of. Instead of people having ideas, it is a case of ideas having people. This is what a manifesto wants to accomplish. From *The Communist Manifesto* by Marx and Engels to Hitler's *Mein Kampf** manifestos are written to make a human being feel small in the face of the grand plans that lie ahead just like a person standing on the threshold of the cathedral in Reims. They may be threatening and apocalyptic or inspirational and world-bettering in intent, but their underlying aim is beside the point. It is the deterministic nature of manifestos ("This Will Happen!") that is the chief concern and the target of this book. It is no wonder that they are seductive. They offer leadership in a time of bewilderment. They offer a "we" in a desert of "me". They are steady handrails in the rickety staircase of time.

But they will lead us astray if we sacrifice the Me on the altar of We, abandon judgment to avoid insecurity and become followers to a leader as blind as ourselves.

---

*   There are in excess of 10,000 titles on Amazon with the word Manifesto.

Blindness, loneliness, bewilderment and insecurity are less enjoyable features of our life but can be powerful triggers of creation, as we shall see in the following chapter.

What a Minifesto Is

The less obvious feature of the Reims cathedral is that even though it is very big, it is built to unleash a power from within you: faith. Building something very large to trigger something small and invisible is counter-intuitive and contrarianism is the central premise of a Minifesto. Where a Manifesto is a document to inspire many people into action, a minifesto is written to inspire only one person – yourself. Where a Manifesto builds on determinism – this will happen! – a minifesto relies on ambiguity – who knows what will happen? Manifestos have exclamation marks, a minifesto has only question marks. Manifestos are explicit, the minifesto is tacit. Manifestos are full of pre-packaged thinking and opinions ready to eat, whilst the minifesto is a cookbook. Manifestos are about pet ideas to bring home and keep in a cage and thereby keep your thinking in a cage. The Minifesto is about wild ideas and going where they roam.

Entering The Muzone

Books about finding new ideas are often about going somewhere else – Silicon Valley, China or Berlin – instead

MINIFESTO

MANIFESTO

of tapping into yourself. Furthermore, we live in a time of constant stimuli – from smartphones offering games, social media apps and click holes* to the hustle of a big city and the smaller cities that try to emulate it. It is, in other words, very difficult to tap into yourself nowadays. We are constantly being told to get an education, get a job, work hard, stay busy, learn constantly and develop, which are recipes to add stimuli to our lives. Some people gain insight and inspiration from cluttered environments but the research done for this book showed something different altogether. Instead of super-motivated entrepreneurs making pilgrimages to Silicon Valley, it showed how creation often came from slightly lost individuals who went where others did not and found ideas within themselves. We can call this place, this inner muse, The *Muzone* – a hybridization of muse and zone. The Muzone can be conjured up at the most unexpected times and locations – dreams, a drunken stupor, bars, porches, cars and just about any place we can think of. The Muzone is a situation more than it is a particular place. The coming chapters will look at examples of people who entered The Muzone with very little in common but who all came out on the other side with something remarkable, an idea that for them changed everything.

---

* A Click Hole, according to *Urban Dictionary*, is like a black hole, but for the internet. One click leads you to the next which leads you to the next which leads into the next. And the next thing you know, eight hours has passed and you don't exactly know how you got where you are.

CHAPTER

FAILUREOLOGY

CUT TO

Jens Spendrup, a down-on-his-luck beer brewer, is sitting with two other guests in the early hours of a midsummer's night birthday party in Sweden in the 1970s.

Luck is a word we tend to use when we do not really know why something happens – Usain Bolt winning a hundred meter race is not luck, whilst picking the right lottery numbers is. "Down-on-his-luck" might be a sloppy description of Spendrup as the causes of his woes are clear, but the description still fits because the causes were out of his hands and the results of unfortunate coincidences.

He had joined the family brewery on a whim in the late 1960s as an accounting intern. His family had been brewers for many generations and the father asked him to help out one summer after graduating from university. This was a turbulent time in Sweden and across Europe. The growth that had blessed the continent for decades after World War II – the years called the *les trente glorieuses* by the French – were coming to an end and a radical leftist wind was blowing across politics. Sweden was in essence a one-party state between 1932 and 1976, ruled by the social democrats, and the country was seen as a role-model in building a sustainable welfare system, helped of course by high economic growth and the fact that the manufacturing capabilities had not been bombed during the war. The early 1970s was a different story altogether, with the oil crash, high inflation and increasing unemployment. The social democrats, high on power after nearly half a century in office and influenced by the leftist winds, came up with bolder and more sinister plans to turn the tide. One of them was to create a brewery monopoly – the government already controlled alcohol distribution – so it started buying up smaller breweries or forcing them out of business. The sales figures and balance sheet for Spendrup's family brewery were not good. When the father fell ill and passed away in the spring of 1976, the company was facing bankruptcy and Spendrup still recalls the ominous feeling of imminent collapse as the books were closed that fall. Alas, he could not escape since the bank forced him to take over his father's loans. He could neither run nor hide but was chained to a sinking ship. The brewery had lost nearly all its restaurant customers but one remained, a small tavern in the remote Swedish countryside. When the owner of the tavern – the sole customer – turned 50 in the summer of 1977, Spendrup decided to attend even though the party was held in the middle of a long-planned family vacation. Instead of going with his wife and children to the in-laws' summerhouse, he went to the party alone and found himself amongst the last few guests sitting together watching the sunrise after a night of food, drinks and dancing. The other two were Carl-Jan Granqvist, a chef and Sven Trägårdh, a sales agent. In a drowsy post-party state, their conversation had ranged from everything to nothing when Trägårdh happened to mention that he was looking for someone who could brew and sell the German brand Löwenbräu on the Swedish market. He had been asking virtually everyone and consciously avoided Spendrup's brewery; they were too small and nearly bankrupt. Spendrup, fuelled by a desire to turn around the misfortune and desperate to try anything or, perhaps just tired and possibly drunk in the early hours, asked Trägårdh to reconsider. After a few meetings with the German brewery giant, at which they fortunately did not inquire about Spendrup's finances, the manufacturing started a year later and sales were conservatively estimated at a few million litres. Instead, Spendrup had to start buying up capacity at other breweries since the projected sales doubled then tripled. What had happened between Trägårdh looking for a licensee in the summer of 1977 and Spendrup's brewery making the beer in 1978 was that Löwenbräu's famous azure label had found its way into the hands of an exciting, edgy young mod singer in London called Rod Stewart. The beer became the lifeblood of cosmopolitan nightlife across Europe. When Spendrup recalls the fortunate coincidence today, he talks about believing in angels: "Somebody up there must have liked us." In the face of certain doom, a door to a different future had opened up.

Failure's Secret

As a public speaker, I face all kinds of audiences and receptions of my message. Some audiences rave and you get a rush from a job well done. Others are quieter but you still feel that they listen intently. Then, occasionally, you have that sort of speaking engagement when both the audience and your speech are off the mark. I had one of those experiences in Sitges in October 2014. The setting was a conference for human resource professionals and I was invited as the after-dinner speaker, which means you are the missing link between dinner and more drinks in the bar afterwards. Almost immediately, I felt that what I had prepared was not up to par. The audience was drunk, ready to dance and have fun and here comes a futurologist with a somewhat serious message about the world. You know you have failed when the response at the end of the speech is short, diplomatic applause. The delegates' evaluation came a week later and contained sentences like "too long", "felt unstructured and rambling" and most painfully, "Not convinced by Magnus, I'm afraid. I got the sense that he could substitute 'HR' for any other profession, dependent on his audience. Felt that he faltered when asked about the future challenges for HR, and answered generically." This is the risk you take as a public speaker – you get up on stage and hope that what you have prepared will resonate with people in a way that inspires and energizes them. When you fail to do so, for whatever reason, it stings, hurts and burns. Sometimes for a long time afterwards. Failure sucks, yet it has a secret that sometimes gets lost as we shrug off the embarrassment and move on. In the case of my Sitges debacle, the secret presented itself later that same evening. As I was standing at the bar to talk with the increasingly drunk delegates, a business journalist introduced himself. Instead of obfuscating his message with polite but insincere compliments about the talk, he cut straight to the chase: "Magnus, you don't really do big ideas, do you?" I asked him what he meant and he answered that he had read my books and now listened to my speech and found that whenever I talk about big changes and trends, his interest faded, yet when I shared small, intimate stories, something happened in him. I understood what he meant and had a moment of clarity. I had lost myself in the imperative to talk about Big, Important Future Trends to the point that I had lost what once drew me to the subject of futurology; a love of human ingenuity and creativity. His criticism was razor-sharp but because it was perfectly valid, did not sting like the "Magnus is boring" comments did in the evaluation. In fact, his comments gave me a path to write this book. Failure's secret is that it brings you to your knees, shames you, silences you, even strips you naked sometimes and then, when you are at your most vulnerable, gives you a building block from which you can start a new journey. Failure sucks, it is what happens after failure that matters or as a football coach put it: "Losing the game does not mean you should lose the lesson." In the case of Jens Spendrup, we saw how near constant adversity had left him vulnerable but also open to new impressions enabling a kind of "revenge".

Positive Revenge

We tend to associate the word "revenge" with negative connotations like an angry payback or "an eye for an eye." There should therefore be a word for "positive revenge" that describes what people do in the wake of failure, when they stick around to learn its secret.

CUT TO

Ray Wagner, president at Mattel Toy Corporation in the 1970s was, according to those that worked with him, a dynamic, smart and all-around impressive man. His passion for toys was transferred to his employees who were urged to consider every aspect of a toy – from packaging and design to marketing and sales. One day, the agent representing a budding filmmaker called George Lucas walks into the Mattel office to pitch a movie about to be released called *Star Wars*. Would Mattel be interested in manufacturing the toys for an upfront fee of $750,000? Wagner declined since he considered movies to be one-off events, like fireworks, whereas a TV show would be shown over and over. The decision turned out to be a mistake when *Star Wars* toys became the most successful merchandise of all time and every kid's must-have Christmas gift for years to come. If the story stopped here, it would be a tale warning us of blinding heuristics and the perils sticking to old knowledge – Wagner's adage that TV shows work better than movies – in the face of a changing world. Instead, the story continues.

In the early 1980s, *Star Wars* figures were one of few toys attracting young boys and the crew at Mattel were hungry for revenge – they needed a line of toys that would have the same appeal to boys as *Barbie* did for girls. They started brainstorming and testing various concepts ranging from army-themed action figures to futuristic space dolls and barbarian-themed toys. The executives experimented by fusing the three concepts together into a futuristic barbarian space army theme. It looked exciting and different. What could they call it? They had used derivative descriptions like "Star Wars 2" or "GI Joe 2" during the development phase of the various themes. There was also a place-holder name that everybody hated: "He-Man." When the prototypes of the figures were presented to senior management at Mattel at a December conference, Ray Wagner was impressed. He pointed to the action figures and said: "Those have the power!" He-Man toys were launched together with a cartoon TV series in 1982 and became some of the most successful toys in the world over the coming years. *He-Man's* catchphrase? "I have the power!" Ray Wagner and Mattel's positive revenge yielded significant results.

CUT TO

Frank Sinatra is singing in a town in Sweden called Finspång, a place so small you have to zoom in very close on Google Maps to find it. It is the early 1950s and only a handful of people have made it to the show. Sinatra had spent the 1940s as a kind of Justin Bieber or One

Direction for his generation singing in front of thousands of screaming fans. Now, he is a 37-year-old washout and standing on a lonely stage in the middle of nowhere was a cruel reminder of fame's fleeting nature. Adding to the cruelty of the situation was the fact that Sinatra had recently lost both his record contracts and his TV show. The performance in Finspång must have been some kind of rock bottom. Many celebrities succumb to drugs and other destructive lifestyles once the cozy warmth of celebrity is replaced by the chilling winds of oblivion. We can only speculate about how close Sinatra was to giving it all up. Instead, his career took a new turn. His wife, actress Ava Gardner, got him an audition as supporting actor in a movie. He had to cut his salary significantly but the movie saved him. Its name was *From Here To Eternity* and it won Sinatra an Academy Award for Best Supporting Actor. Capitol Records signed him, and his music went from the light-hearted but disposable sound he was known for earlier, to an elegiac undertone and a different, more mature, voice. He would go on to make his most famous, long-lived songs during the years with Capitol. The Frank Sinatra that became a legend took nearly 40 years to emerge and had to take a detour via a small town in Sweden.

The Pain of Learning

What the stories of Mattel Toys and Frank Sinatra illustrate is that learning is a two-stage, often painful, process.

Stage one is a shattering of illusions. In the case of Mattel, the belief that films are less attractive as licensing vehicles than TV programs cost the company millions in lost revenue. For Sinatra, what seemed like a career that would last forever ground to a halt – the projected trajectory was broken. Human beings, in general, want to avoid uncertainty, so we cling to assumptions, even though they might be false. When they break down, we feel lost and confused. Stage two in the process is the weary first step in a new, illusionless world, where you do not know true from false and every step becomes a leap into darkness. It is this jump into darkness that is of particular interest as we discern failure's ability to trigger new ideas.

CUT TO

A rock band is trying to make a new album at the Hansa recording studio in Berlin. Their name is U2 and it's the start of the 1990s.

The band had spent the 1980s finding massive success and touring the world, especially America, extensively. They had left their native Ireland as an "interesting post-punk phenomenon" in the early part of the decade and come back to do a New Year's Eve show in their hometown Dublin in 1989. It did not go well. They looked like some big American showband run amok and they even felt themselves that they had become the enemy they so despised when they swore allegiance to punk band The Clash in the late 1970s. Their lead singer Paul "Bono"

Hewson felt that the band they had turned into did not become them. He announced on stage that this was the end of something for the band and that they were now "going away to dream it all up again." They were physically exhausted and felt that they had run out of steam creatively. It was not just a case of having to make corrective adjustments; everything they had become would have to go.

The feeling of wanting to break with the past is common in artists that have found success, which is why rock bands tend to split up and members go in different directions citing the clichéd "creative differences" as a cause for the divorce. U2 stuck together but became a divided band. Bono and the guitarist Dave "The Edge" Evans were into new kinds of dance music like Happy Mondays and experimental machine age outfits like KMFDM and Einsturzende Neubaten. The drummer, Larry Mullen Jr, got into old school rock and jazz music while the bassist, Adam Clayton, started drinking heavily. They were hoping that Berlin would enable them to focus on a new album with a new kind of sound in a city where a culture clash was happening after the fall of the Berlin Wall and the beginnings of a new Europe. The choice of recording studio was also symbolic since Hansa Studios was where David Bowie and Iggy Pop had been reborn creatively when they had hit dead-ends.

It was not to be. U2 ran into a wall. They had no finished songs, just a lot of conflicting ideas and unfinished demos. The atmosphere was burdened with tension, doubt and every member retreated into his own space, betraying the concept of a group. Most damagingly, no new songs were coming out of the sessions. The idea of U2 splitting up must have crossed minds several times during the recording.

One October day, they spent a long time jamming to one of the demo tapes they had written called *Sick Puppy*. The song used a pumping bass line and looped drum machine to generate a sound very different from the kind of Americana rock that U2 had become known for in the 1980s. Bono was ad-libbing words on top and The Edge was coming up with guitar loops. Twenty minutes into the jam, Bono called for a new, improvised bridge – the snippet of music between verse and chorus – and seemingly from out of nowhere, a series of chords emerged: A minor, D, F and G. Suddenly something very powerful was happening in the room. As Bono later described it: "Something happens … something comes into the room and you know it, everyone knew it … it was one of those hairs on the back of your neck moment." They stopped jamming and started writing a song on the basis of those four chords. What emerged was *One*, which became the keystone for the upcoming album *Achtung Baby* and also one of U2's most successful singles ever*. The song is credited with saving the band as they faced creative

---

* *Sick Puppy* would later be called *Mysterious Ways* and also became a hit single.

bankruptcy in Berlin. The producer, Mark "Flood" Ellis, says that recording an album is "fraught with danger because you can fail at any one moment but that's the beauty of it, if you remove the safety net and are prepared to really expose yourselves. Your pursuit is after the magic moments, those moments of 'wow, I would never have imagined ...'". Bono is more blunt about the transformation the band underwent: "You have to reject one expression of the band first before you get to the next and in between, you have nothing. You have to risk it all." Nothingness is what failure can produce and it unlocked the Muzone for U2.

Nothing

U2 did not just kill their darlings, they committed a veritable *darlingcide* where everything they had stood for and worked hard to achieve was thrown out the window in favour of finding new ideas from which to build from. This is something few people – in the music industry or beyond – are willing to do. Not because we do not want new ideas but because the idea of nothing – having nothing and being nothing – is genuinely frightening. If you put the stories of this chapter side by side, they are united by nothingness – Jens Spendrup facing imminent bankruptcy, Mattel missing out on *Star Wars* toys, Frank Sinatra abandoned in Finspång and me in Sitges. When we let go of our beliefs, we liberate a creative spark. Failure makes us vulnerable and if we allow that vulnerability to make us open to new ideas, it can serve as a basis for something new and different. Nothingness is not only frightening, it is also very difficult to achieve. We live cluttered lives, full of meetings, music, films, conversations and plans. Very rarely do we find ourselves in the silence of nothing. The British philosopher Robert Rowland Smith puts it as follows: "If you keep yourself topped off with ideas all the time, you never become open enough to get the sustenance you require in order to move on. You end up just recycling what is already in the *zeitgeist*." Just like anti-matter is the opposite of matter in physics, the Muzone is a kind of anti-place, where we cannot go at will and cannot locate on a map. It can just happen to us in these inflection points of nothingness. Failure, in particular its tendency to crush our beliefs, opens up that anti-place in all of us. The price we pay can be high – some never recover from failure – but it is a risk we must be willing to take if we want to find something new beyond the horizon.

There is, however, something strange about the Muzone. Although it is triggered by nothingness, it is full of things that were already in us: memories, experiences, fragmented ideas and impressions. It is as if we have a secret chamber hiding in our psyche. This chamber and its contents is the subject of the next chapter.

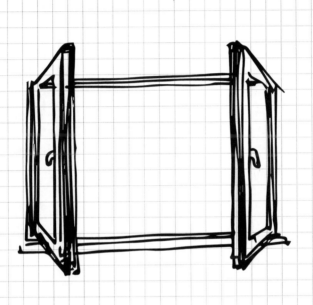

CHAPTER 6

SOUVENIRS FROM THE GREAT BEYOND

CUT TO

You are in the passenger seat of a car travelling on a northern Florida highway one night in the mid-1950s. The engine is beating and the radio crackles with whatever music was on the charts back then. The driver is getting drunk. His name is James McLamore and a few miles back in Jacksonville, at a doors-falling-off-the-hinges kind of restaurant, he happened to taste the most divine hamburger. It was so good that he is now gulping whiskey-laced 7-Up and reconstructing the burger in his head. Licking his lips. Mmmm'ing. Taking a sip every now and then from his improvised cocktail. Miraculously, McLamore neither crashes the car nor gets arrested for driving under the influence on this particular night. Instead, he will recreate this perfect burger in Miami, call it *The Whopper*, and lay the foundation for what is today Burger King.

The Real Meaning of Life

There is something truly magical about consciousness. On the one hand, it is a lens through which we perceive reality using our five senses. On the other hand, it seems to work like a portal through which we can tap into altered states of emotion, find new ideas and explore other worlds. Philosopher Sam Harris has described the meaning of life as a continuous quest to alter your mind using various means: "Everything we do is for the purpose of altering consciousness. We form friendships so that we can feel certain emotions, like love, and avoid others, like loneliness. We eat specific foods to enjoy their fleeting presence on our tongues. We read for the pleasure of thinking another person's thoughts. Every waking moment – and even in our dreams – we struggle to direct the flow of sensation, emotion, and cognition toward states of consciousness that we value."

There is a range of tools – legal and illegal – at our disposal if we seek to experiment with our consciousness. Jim McLamore used alcohol, which is quite common. Author Jack Kerouac explained his alcoholism, which ended up killing him, as follows: "As I grew older I became a drunk. Why? Because I like the ecstasy of the mind."

Love is another tool. When we say love is blind, what we really mean is that love – like alcohol – can seriously skew our judgment in negative ways. Music is a third tool and journalist John Seabrook has a beautiful, vivid explanation of why so many of us prefer walking around a city with Spotify in our headphones instead of listening to the noise around us: "Ordinary domestic life needs its bliss points, those moments of transcendence throughout the day – that just-behind-the-eyelids sense of quivering possibility that at any moment the supermarket aisle might explode into candy-coloured light. The hooks promise that pleasure. But the ecstasy is fleeting, and like snack food it leaves you feeling unsatisfied, always craving just a little more." Let us zoom in on those "moments of transcendence" Seabrook describes. The dictionary describes transcendent as: "going beyond the limits of ordinary experience" and "far better or greater than what is usual" – a perfect description of McLamore's Jacksonville hamburger. Seeking experiences that are out of the ordinary are the reason people travel, but also the reason why travel sometimes lets us down. Silicon Valley in California, for example, has developed a reputation as the world capital of digital entrepreneurship. We constantly read about robots, self-driving cars and billion-dollar companies being formed in Palo Alto garages and imagine that the future has somehow already arrived on the West Coast of the United States. Yet when I visited the place over a few months in 2013, it was a big let-down. It looks like any ordinary American suburbia, full of office parks, shopping malls and pricey yet unremarkable real estate. Even famous places like the garage where technology firm Hewlett & Packard was created looked like, well, just another garage. When we speak of Silicon Valley – or other famous destinations that pique our imagination – we are really talking about a place beyond what we can see.

How to write a global hit song in only two hours

CUT TO

Jazz singer Amy Winehouse is recording a new album with producer Mark Ronson in New York in 2006. Winehouse spent so long procrastinating in writing a follow-up to her modestly successful debut album *Frank* that her record label has considered dropping her. Now, she is on fire and needs only two or three hours writing a new song called *Back to Black*. This became the title track of the 2007 breakthrough album that made her a global superstar. Mark Ronson was astonished that the song – lyrics and melody – took only a few hours to write. The reality is, of course, that Back to Black took many years to write. Winehouse had from a young age been blessed with a unique singing voice as well as remarkable charisma. She had been singing professionally since the early 2000s. Most importantly – and perhaps tragically – the song gained its emotional resonance from a failed, destructive relationship with her boyfriend that had ended a year earlier leaving Winehouse in a state of misery. What Winehouse's song – along with all artistic expression that moves us – represents, is a kind of compressed experience that had been brewing, soaking and biding its time to finally emerge like a diamond from charcoal. Her heartbreak must have been hell to live through, but it generated an emotional space for Winehouse to explore that, in turn, resonated with millions of listeners around the world. We often make the mistake of looking at what we can see – two hours of song writing, two people in a Silicon Valley garage or an apple falling on Newton's head – when we seek to understand how creation happens. This is why a flashing light bulb is the most common – and misleading – way of illustrating how ideas happen. To understand creation, we should consider the compression process – how years of living with all the dead ends, mistakes, heartbreak and turmoil it entails, translate into a short moment where pen is put to paper and the magic happens. To illustrate this, consider a Croatian cartoon called *Balthazaar* that aired in the 1970s. Every episode would present the professor with some kind of problem to solve and he ended up walking in circles for hours to think about a solution. Finally, he activated his magic machine, full of pipes, valves and – because this was the 70s – hallucinogenic visual effects. The machine got to work – lights were flashing, colours streaming and steam blowing – and at the very end produced three magical drops that the professor could use to solve the problem – compressed, packaged experience in action.

From Blip to Bing

Singer Katy Perry got the phrase "I kissed a girl and I liked it" in a dream and put it into her global hit song. The inventor of the lava lamp and the inventor of the pet rock, a successful 1970s novelty toy, were both drunk in bars when the ideas came to them. Film director James Cameron was delirious in a fever he got from food poisoning when he got the idea about a killer cyborg called a Terminator. Entrepreneur Stewart Butterfield also got his idea for Flickr, a famous photo sharing website, when he was up vomiting all night because of food poisoning. And so on. Drunkenness, dreaming and food poisoning are not the normal places where you would look for ideas but they are tremendously effective in opening The Muzone. So why don't more sick people, drunks or dreamers become successful entrepreneurs, filmmakers or artists? What separates the many blips – random insights, ideas and impressions – we encounter in a day from the "bing" of an idea that we develop into something greater? The answer is that Flickr, "I kissed a girl", The Terminator, The Lava Lamp and The Pet Rock were not just random thoughts landing from above – they were tools on a path their creators were already on. Going back to the example of Amy Winehouse, her heartbreak must have seemed meaningless and painful when it happened but the fact that she was an artist enabled her to turn the experience into a tool when writing her new album. James Cameron, Katy Perry, Stewart Butterfield and the others were already on a path – to make a movie, write a song and start a company – when the solutions came to them in dreams and disorientation. What distinguishes random events from meaningful ones is the path we put them on. This will become clear in the next story.

How a failed herbicide saved children's lives

CUT TO

The late 1980s and Elisabeth Holme, a doctor at Sahl-grenska Hospital in Gothenburg, Sweden, taking a drag from a cigarette. She smoked all the time. Those who knew her describe her as somewhat odd – even strange – but with a razor-sharp intellect. She had a very close professional relationship with her more congenial colleague, Professor Sven Lindstedt, and together they were studying a rare disease afflicting children called Tyrosinaemia. The disease is a genetic disorder that prevents the body from breaking down a basic building block of protein called tyrosine. This, in turn, leads to a build up of waste products in the body and the children die of liver failure. A child's death is not just a tragedy. For a doctor, it is a professional failure and when your patients keep dying from the same disease over and over again, it leads to deep frustration.

Meanwhile, on the other side of the world in Australia, an agrochemical company had discovered an interesting feature in the Bottle Brush Plant. The plant thrives in the southern hemisphere and is stunning when in bloom and can live in a variety of different climates, from tropical to cool temperatures. The interesting feature Zeneca Agrochemicals had discovered was that nothing grew underneath the plant's branches, as if they contained some kind of natural herbicide. Further research showed that this was precisely the case and the company proceeded to patent the herbicide molecule called Nitisinone. Unfortunately, the molecule had a nasty surprise in store that would ruin the entire business case for Zeneca: When they tested Nitisinone, or NTCB to use its chemical acronym, it made mice go blind. First, their eyes would become cloudy, then the vision would disappear completely. Zeneca were curious to understand exactly why. Additional experimentation showed that NTCB inhibited an enzyme found in all living organisms called HPPD. When they started researching the field of HPPD-inhibitors, they stumbled upon work done in a completely different field, far away from Australia. It turned out that HPPD was one of the key destructive elements in a rare disease called Tyrosinemia. When Doctors Holme and Lindstedt read about the research in a science journal, they moved quickly to do small trials at the hospital. In the development of pharmaceuticals within rare diseases, you cannot do expensive, large-scale clinical trials for the obvious reason that there are not enough patients. To some extent, this is also a blessing enabling faster development. Holme and Lindstedt obtained a quantity of NTCB – intended as herbicide – to treat a seriously ill two-month-old child in the winter of 1991. Even in the conservatively worded scientific journal that later described the treatment, the language cannot conceal amazement: "The outcome of the treatment was dramatic … the liver function rapidly returned to normal … and the patient has been able to lead a fairly normal life." The failed herbicide became a miracle drug called Orfadin, saving the lives of countless children around the world.

The lesson of this example is that a path – in this case, being on a quest to save your infant patients – can make seemingly random events – the chemical processes of a herbicide on the other side of the world – valuable tools. As human beings, we read, hear and see things all the time. Any one of these things can be a gateway to greater discoveries, greater wealth or greater well-being yet they pass us by because we have not defined what path we are on. Then again, sometimes the path only becomes clear in hindsight and the tools we have gathered were found haphazardly as we were strolling along.

Askeladden

Every culture around the world has myths that resonate deeply with and reflect those who cultivate them. In Norway, one of those myths is about Askeladden, the youngest of three siblings. His older brothers Per and Pål plan, strategize and are seen as the designated winners whereas Askeladden is a happy-go-lucky character who stumbles on things along the way. In one of the most celebrated fairy tales featuring the three brothers, Per and Pål vow to get the hand of the princess, who is symbolically placed on a slippery glass mountain. Askeladden, meanwhile, just kind of walks around and finds seemingly random things. Per and Pål chase the most direct route to the heart of the princess but guess who wins? This fairy tale has come to symbolize Norway's tendency to stumble upon the future be it discovering oil in the North Sea or forgetting to invest the oil riches enabling them to make the largest purchase of equities ever in the wake of the 2008 financial crisis and thereby creating the world's richest sovereign wealth fund. The Askeladden way of achieving your goals through indirect means has a fancier name: obliquity. Economist John Kay, who has written a book on the subject, claims that "the most profitable companies are not the most profit-oriented, and the happiest people are not those who make happiness their main aim." This is a different kind of approach to strategy. Many of us seem to believe that the best way of curing a disease, writing a hit song or creating a valuable company is to focus intently on the problem at hand but it turns out that failures in other industries, troubled personal relationships and things like food poisoning can be more effective catalysts.

Everything we encounter, suffer through and stumble upon in life can contribute to some greater goal but we might not know what or when. Take the decision in 1541 by strict Christian reformist John Calvin to ban jewellery in the city of Geneva. Calvin and the Calvinist interpretation of Catholicism that he founded wanted to strip away all the superficial glitz from society with a battle cry of "*Sola Fide* (Faith Alone) – *Sola Scriptura*

(Scripture Alone)." No longer would the skilled jewellery makers be allowed to practice or display their craft. At around the same time in France, the protestant Huguenots were persecuted, massacred and driven out of the country. Many of them settled in the Jura region of eastern Switzerland where they practiced their craft of making pocket watches. Calvin saw the watches as practical instruments and did not subject them to the jewellery ban, thus unwittingly creating a loophole for the jewellers of Geneva who went on to ally themselves with the exiled Huguenot watchmakers. The family-run companies that emerged from Geneva to Basel, or Watch Valley as it is known today, have become household names: Rolex, Corum, Gallet, Girard-Perregaux, Movado, Patek Philippe, Breitling, TAG Heuer, Tissot, Ulysse Nardin, Chopard and many others. Most management books on innovation herald freedom from demands and deadlines as the key to creativity, yet the history of Swiss watchmaking shows how constraints, legislation and persecution can be conducive to creating something remarkable.

Everything Counts

My father is an entrepreneur with a mixed track record. He found success in the 1980s by building a telephone book empire that he sold. He made millions and intended to spend the rest of his life in semi-retirement. Instead, his fortune was embezzled by a business associate and, for many years, I watched him trying to salvage what was left of the money, failing constantly along the way. The low point came in the early 2000s when he was forced to sell off the country house that he had inherited from his father had hoped would stay in the family for many generations. When he told me about the sale, it was the only time in the whole ordeal that I saw him weep, silently and unceremoniously at a McDonald's restaurant in the middle of Stockholm. He was back to square one – older and wiser but also disillusioned and somewhat resigned. As his oldest son, I had grown up with a sense of mission to make my father whole again and when I saw him in this state, I wanted to cheer him up so I took him on a study tour of India. For ten days, we travelled from Delhi to Bangalore and Mumbai. We met companies, universities, scholars and business people to get a sense of this exciting new continent, the I of the rising BRIC countries.

One of the people we encountered was a Pakistani professor who acted as our guide. As the study tour concluded, he told us about another trip he was planning later that year to China. I was unable to go so my father went on his own. He was dazzled by what he saw – the rapid development of cities, factories, trade and living standards. One of his many failures back in Sweden had been a dental implant company that had recently gone bankrupt. He saw an opportunity to try the same business again but this time using Chinese manufacturing. The company he founded would go on to be his first success in over 20 years. To paraphrase John Milton's poem *Paradise Lost*, long and hard is the road, which from darkness leads up to the light, but if we look closely in the darkness, we will discover things lying on the side of the road that can help us.

When we see the world and its future through a lens of grand narratives, we make the assumption that we are well-equipped to evaluate what we see around us: *that* is a valuable, useful idea while *that* is a meaningless idea. In reality, we simply do not know whether things happening right now are good or bad, where they might take us and what they can lead to. Driving drunk, losing a fortune, heartache and feeding herbicide to babies are not exactly recipes but they teach us that out of misery something good can come. The next chapter will teach us a skill to start seeing random events differently. This chapter closes with a poem by 13th century Persian poet Jalal al-din Rumi entitled *The Guesthouse*:

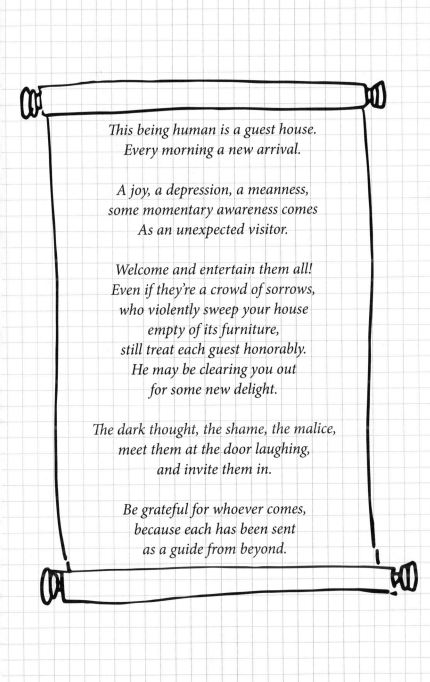

This being human is a guest house.
Every morning a new arrival.

A joy, a depression, a meanness,
some momentary awareness comes
As an unexpected visitor.

Welcome and entertain them all!
Even if they're a crowd of sorrows,
who violently sweep your house
empty of its furniture,
still treat each guest honorably.
He may be clearing you out
for some new delight.

The dark thought, the shame, the malice,
meet them at the door laughing,
and invite them in.

Be grateful for whoever comes,
because each has been sent
as a guide from beyond.

CHAPTER

SEEING WHAT COULD BE

CUT TO

John Walker, a surgeon's apprentice and hobby chemist in the English city Stockton-on-Tees, stirring chemicals in a pot at home in the early 19th century. He came from a good upbringing and was well-educated, even to the point where people would call him "Stockton's encyclopaedia". One of the things that fascinated him was fire and how to control it. At this point in history, lighting candles was a cumbersome exercise where you would first have to build a fire and then find a twig of suitable length with which you could light the kinds of tallow candles people used at home. Walker's dream was to create some kind of instant flame that would ignite quickly and then burn long enough to light a candle. He kept mixing various substances to find the right combustible mix. One day in 1826, he was mixing potassium chlorate and antimony sulphide and found that the gooey paste stuck to the wooden stirring rod. When he tried to scrape it off against the stone floor, it burst into flames. Walker had invented the world's first friction match or, as he called them, "sulphuretted peroxide strikables." Walker was on a path – finding an instant flame with which to light candles – but the actual solution landed on – or rather stuck to – him from seemingly out of the blue. We tend to refer to such moments as accidents or serendipitous events, which belittles the effort of the John Walkers of the world by insinuating that the solution could have landed on anyone, anywhere. This chapter will look closer at what actually happens when these seemingly random events end up producing groundbreaking inventions.

Moments of Mutation

The origin of mankind was for centuries described as a master plan by an omniscient creator. This view has progressively been replaced – with the exception of some conservative elements in the mid-Western United States – with the theory of evolution, wherein humans and other species slowly evolved over millions of years. Even though many people subscribe to the evolutionary theory of human development, they still get one thing wrong: they assume evolution is a path we followed. The mistaken view is understandable given the many textbooks and museums featuring timelines where *homo erectus* and *Neanderthals* seemingly transformed into *homo sapiens* over night. What really unfolded is trickier to get your head around and therefore less suitable to the pedagogic level of schools and natural history museums: Mutations happen all the time, everywhere, in every species. Most are meaningless and do not get noticed. Some are fatal. Others just disfiguring and disabling. What Charles Darwin and other researchers argued when championing the evolutionary view of creation was that some mutations – arguably an infinitesimal amount – lead to some kind of advantage in adapting to the surroundings or in procreation. White fur may help camouflage a rabbit when the climate grows colder and snowier, for example, or an extra large feather plume may attract females to a higher degree in the peacock kingdom. These mutations are very rare but probably did not happen just once. A white rabbit amongst a group of brown ones would likely have gotten killed or, at least, rejected. To understand evolution we must add a longer timeframe than we can readily grasp. If we add millions of years into the mix, we can see how rare mutations, mostly meaningless ones, would occasionally affect the same species twice – like the white rabbit fur – and over many generations grow to become the genetic norm. Given that most books about evolution are very long, it is hard to do the concept more justice than this in a short paragraph. The point is that mutations happen all the time and most lead nowhere. What John Walker's invention exemplifies is a moment of mutation: the paste he has mixed reaches the right balance for combustion and he happens to strike it against the floor. Moments of mutation happen when expected outcomes take an unexpected turn or when some everyday moment – a lazy stroll in the park – is blessed by some surprising event and becomes a portal of discovery.

Discovery versus Invention

We tend to divide discoverers and inventors into two different groups. The former travels to distant places where she scrapes dust off fossils while the latter is seen as a lab-dwelling nerd with a light bulb over her

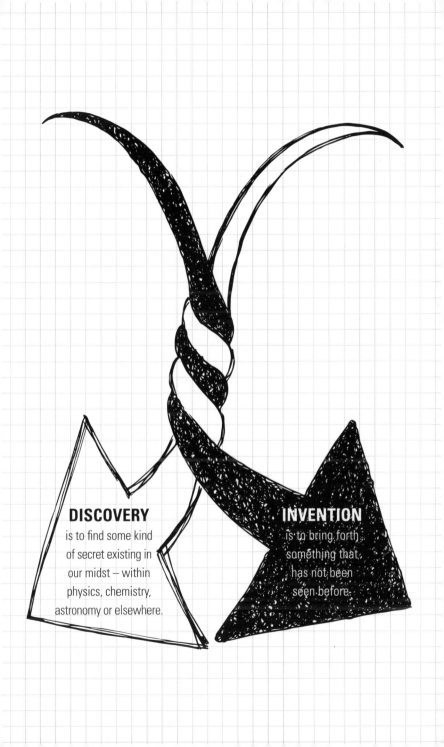

DISCOVERY is to find some kind of secret existing in our midst – within physics, chemistry, astronomy or elsewhere.

INVENTION is to bring forth something that has not been seen before.

head. This division makes us lose sight of the fact that the two concepts – discovery and invention – are intertwined and joined at the hip. To discover is to find some kind of secret existing in our midst – within physics, chemistry, astronomy or elsewhere. To invent is to bring forth something that has not been seen before. Cesar Hidalgo, a researcher at Massachusetts Institute of Technology, distinguishes between an apple and Apple computer. Apples exist in the real world before they exist in people's heads, whereas Apple computers exist first in people's heads before they exist in the real world. Apples were discovered whereas Apple Computer was invented. This distinction is straightforward but easily becomes blurry. Every component within an Apple device was discovered – from the silicone enabling computer processors to the rare earth metals enabling the modern battery. Similarly, apples may have grown on trees for millions of years but it took a human mind to realize they can be a source of nutrition, a commodity on which to make money or something you could glaze with sugar and turn into candy. Acts of creation are a blend of discovery and invention. Take the following example:

CUT TO

A bedridden musician called Brian Eno. He suffered an automobile accident in 1975 and was left temporarily disabled and feverish so he spent his days struggling to reach his turntable and listen to some music as a small consolation. One day, he put on an album of eighteenth-century harp music and returned to bed. Once there, he discovered that his speakers had broken or that the music was turned down too low. Either way, the sound was hovering around the threshold of inaudibility and as he lacked the strength to get out of bed and see what was wrong, he was left to listen through the album this way. It presented a completely new way of hearing music for Eno. Instead of having the songs as an active component in the foreground they blended together with the background, just like the sound of rain or the colours of the wall. It became part of the general ambience, and when Eno got better, he started to experiment with a new type of sound he called *ambient*, launching a revolutionary album called *Discreet Music* in 1975. In this example, we see the moment of mutation – the music being turned down too low and possibly a broken speaker – and how it triggers the blend of discovery and invention. Harp music had been around for centuries yet turning the volume down very low was only possible when the modern stereo had been created. The key to discovery and invention is identifying the moment of mutation as it passes us by.

Making moments of mutation

CUT TO

Andre Geim, a physics professor, had won the "IgNobel Prize" for the silliest science experiment when he showed how to levitate a frog using magnets. He enjoyed this kind of humorous experimentation so he started hosting a Friday afternoon session where he and his colleagues at the University of Manchester played around and did things you are really not supposed to do at a serious academic institution. Geim used one of these sessions to study Graphite, the micro-thin layers of carbon used in pencils or tennis rackets. He and a doctoral student wanted to see how thin they could make the material without destroying it and the student, Da Jiang of China, started polishing a one-inch graphite crystal. It took a few weeks but they finally had a tiny speck of carbon in a petri dish – "a grain of sand from a mountain", as Geim called it. They used sticky tape to test the adhesiveness of the material – this was a fun, free experimental session so anything went – and made a remarkable discovery: under an electron microscope they saw the first two-dimensional layer of carbon ever witnessed, like hexagons in a honeycomb pattern. What was striking too was that the material existed at room temperature. The name of the material was Graphene, which is a hundred times stronger than steel, can conduct heat and energy and is super-light. It is widely seen as one of the most revolutionary materials ever discovered and won Geim a real Nobel prize. He remains the only researcher who has won both the IgNobel for silliness and The Nobel for valuable contributions to humanity. About his Friday sessions, he says: "[It was all about] curiosity-driven research. Something random, simple, maybe a bit weird – even ridiculous …without it, there are no discoveries."

What Geim's sessions illustrate is the importance of play – seeing the world through a lens of humour and fun. If you want to make moments of mutation, or at least set up the preconditions necessary for them to happen, it is a good idea to make the experience enjoyable so that people will want to be in the moment, and not escape from it. This is a stark contrast to serious, dull conferences debating weighty themes and the innovation departments of big corporations expecting a return on investment. We seem to be under the spell of an illusion that says big, important ideas must come from serious, important settings when the example of Graphene, indeed this entire book, wants to show how frivolity, silliness and fun might be better tools. To paraphrase Shakespeare's Duke Orsino in *The Twelfth Night*: "If Fun Be The Food of Discovery, Play On!"

Debunking Luck

If you want to offend a successful person, you should use the word "luck" to describe their accomplishments. Says renowned actor Peter Dinklage: "I hate that word

– 'lucky.' It cheapens a lot of hard work. Living in Brooklyn in an apartment without any heat and paying for dinner at the bodega with dimes – I don't think I felt myself lucky back then. Doing plays for 50 bucks and trying to be true to myself as an artist and turning down commercials where they wanted a leprechaun*. Saying I was lucky negates the hard work I put in and spits on that guy who's freezing his ass off back in Brooklyn. So I won't say I'm lucky. I'm fortunate enough to find or attract very talented people. For some reason I found them, and they found me." Dinklage is right to be upset about the L-word; not only does it belittle his efforts, it also misinterprets what is happening when people find the ideas, the collaborators or the circumstances that make them successful. To illustrate, let us have a look at the following example about a famous invention:

CUT TO

Richard James was a naval engineer in the early 1940s whose job entailed securing instruments on boats against the constant movement of the ocean. One of the key ingredients in doing this was spiral-shaped torsion springs. One day he accidentally knocked a spring over and saw something remarkable – the spring could walk. It moved as if it had a life of its own, flipping over and taking steps forward. After some experimenting, he found a lighter steel material that would enable the spring to

---

*   Dinklage has dwarfism.

climb stairs, as if by magic. The walking inspired the mechanism's name: "Slinky" and James sold over a hundred million of the toys in the coming two years. It is easy to fall into the luck-trap in this story and focus on James's elbow accidentally knocking over the spring, but what really matters is not the accident but what he saw and his tenacity in transforming the moment into a marketable product. He saw both what was there – a torsion spring behaving unexpectedly – and what could be – a toy. This touches a profound truth about the world of ideas. On the one hand, ideas are figments of the imagination, a visualization of the world as it should be, almost like a lie. On the other hand, ideas are observations made in and conclusions drawn from the real world. All the words we have to describe idea-generating exercises are skewed toward seeing ideas as imaginative visions: "blue-skying", "ideation", "brain-storming" all describe a from-the-inside-out approach. When people observe the world to gain ideas – the outside-in approach – we drop the imaginative element and use dry descriptions like "market research" or "empirical study". Therefore, we need a word to describe both.

Seeing What Is and Seeing What Could Be

A battle has raged in the history of philosophy between thinkers who argue that we see the world for what it is and that the world exists objectively outside our minds and thinkers who argue that everything is shaped by

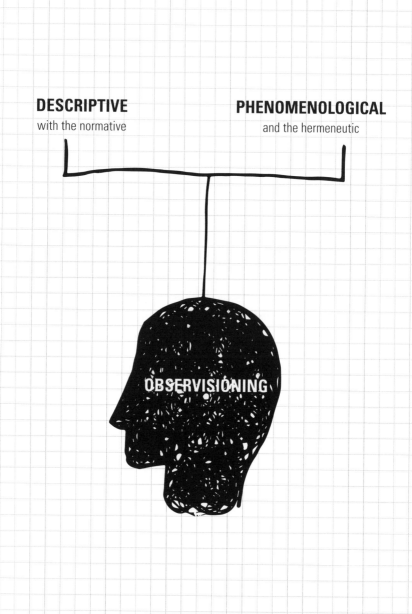

DESCRIPTIVE
with the normative

PHENOMENOLOGICAL
and the hermeneutic

OBSERVISIONING

our judgment and our way of seeing things. This debate carries over from philosophy into the world of social science, where the division is between the descriptive – observing what is without passing judgment – and the normative – arguing that there is a correct, desirable and normal way to proceed. The division between objective description and judgmental observation is obvious in situations where we want to evaluate, not just describe, historical events. Yes, the Nazis did take over Germany in the 1930s, but what should Germany have done instead? Yes, the global banking system did collapse in 2008, but what should the regulators and bank managers have done instead? The objective approach is easily accused of nihilism – void of any moral compass – whereas the normative approach is often accused of revisionism – rewriting history and falsifying facts. If we were to make peace between these dichotomies, we would need a word that united the descriptive with the normative, the phenomenological and the hermeneutic. The word would be a hybrid between observation – seeing what is – and envisioning – seeing what could be. That word would be *observisioning*.

Observisioning in Action

All technology begins as a simple trick. The first mobile phones were heavy bricks with which we could only make brief, expensive telephone calls announcing our arrival time or bragging that we made the call from our car. To imagine that these bricks would one day contain social media tools and video would have been impossible. The first pages we surfed on the World Wide Web had grey background and black text with no hint of the e-commerce or file-sharing capabilities to come. The first motion picture ever made was called "Monkeyshines" and was a short snippet made in 1889 of a ghostly white figure flashing for a few minutes. To see it and imagine that this medium would one day become a billion dollar industry and a powerful cultural tool would have been unfathomable. Yet observisioning is exactly that – seeing what is and imagining what could be. This is not a matter of merely extrapolating – draw a straight line and the the brick-like mobile phones would only become more brick-like and movies would forever be short, plotless snippets. Observisioning is about understanding the hidden, secret potential of an object, technology or idea. Richard James's torsion spring was just a spare part, but he saw a toy. Brian Eno's stereo was broken but he heard a new musical genre emerging. The prophecies about the internet sounded crazy when we slowly downloaded the grey web pages of the early 1990s, yet they came true.

Observisioning is a leap of faith wherein we risk having others accuse us of being crazy. "There is nothing in a caterpillar that tells you it's going to be a butterfly" as architect Buckminster Fuller stated in the 1950s. He might as well have been describing the art of observisioning.

CUT TO

Alberto "Beto" Pérez, a Colombian fitness instructor, was late to his aerobics class and had forgotten the CD of aerobics music. Drawing a deep sigh, he was forced to improvise and use one of his personal mix-tapes featuring salsa, meringue and other rhythms of South America. The aerobics class loved it. He named the crossover concept *Zumba* and it grew out of Colombia to become a global phenomenon reaching millions of participants in over a hundred countries worldwide.

CUT TO

A broken car stereo in a suburb of Stockholm. Behind the wheel is Swedish DJ and music producer Dag Volle or, as everyone calls him, Denniz Pop. He spends his days working in a small studio called Swemix that he built with some colleagues, and artists from all over Sweden send him demo tapes asking for a dance-floor friendly remix by the Swemix collective. When the car stereo breaks down one day in 1991, it forces him to listen to the same demo tape over and over again. It is made by a Gothenburg quartet and features a hideous blend of synth-laced reggae sung by two women whose grasp of the English language is, diplomatically speaking, limited. Volle plays the song to a friend and they both laugh at how bad it is. Nevertheless, he is forced to endure the tape for nearly a week until the stereo is repaired. It is during that time that something about the demo strikes him, like something inside the amateur-ish music aching to get out – a beat, a sound, an idea. Instead of ridiculing the songs, Volle decides that he wants to produce a single with the four-piece. He calls them up, invites them to Stockholm and they quickly produce a song that no Swedish record label wants to release. So Swemix launch it with a label from Denmark. The result is called *All That She Wants* by the band Ace of Base, one of the most successful hit singles of 1993 and whose follow-up debut album, *The Sign*, would become one of the most successful albums in the world ever.

Accidents and mistakes are things we seek to avoid in life. We invent proverbs, like "to err is human", and read self-help books to help us rise above these ordeals. When we are asked, we usually shrug off the experience and mumble something about how they taught us a lesson or made us stronger, all the while treating them like something we are a bit ashamed of. What this chapter has shown is that these moments of mutation – when expected became unexpected – are catalysts to creative thinking. John Walker, the inventor of matches, was living through an exciting time in the history of the modern economy. The Enlightenment had stirred up an interest in scientific discovery. Villages around Europe were full of tinkering individuals who would, merely as a hobby, experiment in chemistry, physics, materials and beyond. Remember that Walker was a surgeon's apprentice by day and consider how many medical students today dabble in electric engineering or computer programming on the side? Not many. With rising complexity comes a greater specialization that, in turn, closes down the amateur movement so influential in pioneering discoveries in the 1800s. Instead of amateurs, we have silos of specialization today. Instead of tinkering, we have large budgets and business objectives. Instead of play, we have big, serious challenges. Yet ideas – big, small, stupid or smart – require play, improvisation, experimentation and a whole lot of failures to succeed. We would do well to *observision* how these failures can translate into something new, different and better.

CHAPTER

WE-DEAS

CUT TO

Boxing ring announcer Michael Buffer grabs the microphone to kick-start the next match. He clears his throat discreetly and lets his mighty tenor shake through the PA:

"Fasten your seatbelts and man your battle stations!"

The audience ignores him.

Buffer's intended kick-start moment fizzles out.

He had landed this role as a fluke after a career in modelling and he spent a few years doing a pedestrian job, frustrated by his inability to trigger a sense of excitement at the opening of boxing matches. Then, one day in the early 1980s, he remembers something the legendary boxer Muhammad Ali would say before his fights a decade earlier: "Oh, I'm so pretty... I'm ready to rumble, rumble, rumble..."

Buffer fine-tunes Ali's catchphrase and creates five words that have become synonymous with the start of big, loud, sporting events: "Let's get ready to rumble!"

What is remarkable is that the phrase has netted Michael Buffer nearly half a billion dollars in royalty payments and merchandise. It is an entertaining thought to imagine parental advice or career counselling along the lines of: "Son, do not bother with that long, fancy education degree – just come up with five words that will make you a fortune."

CUT TO

A frustrated *hausfrau* in Germany in the early 1900s. Being a housewife, we can only assume that there are myriad causes of her frustrations yet on this particular day, it is the difficulty of making coffee that draws her ire. The coffee pots, called percolators, were prone to over-brew the coffee, whereas the espresso-type machines would leave ground in the drink and the linen bag filter – similar to tea bags – were a chore to clean afterwards. Her frustrations made her experiment with new ways of making coffee. She ended up taking some blotting paper from her son, making holes in a brass pot using a nail and letting the coffee filter through the paper, through the perforated pot and into a kettle. The result was a ground-free, less bitter coffee. Her name was Melitta Bentz and her solution would become known to the world as Melitta filters.

The stories of Michael Buffer and Melitta Bentz are archetypal in that they focus on a single individual who, through a moment of inspiration, finds an idea that they cultivate. Joseph Campbell, a professor of mythology, has coined the concept of the *monomyth* – the hero's journey – in which a character gets a call to action, goes into the wilderness to reach some kind of revelation, and then comes back into our world to bless us with his finding.

It is called a monomyth because Campbell believed all narratives – from Shakespeare to *Star Wars* – are variations of this story. We can see how the stories of Bentz and Buffer neatly fit this template. Finding ideas is often described as a solo sport and there are indeed many examples where this description is accurate. Yet there is another way of viewing ideas not as isolated objects, or sunflowers, but as social constructs intertwined with many people, like bougainvillea. Like love, humour or bad breath, these ideas are defined by the spaces between us.

The Crusade

Our surroundings make us who we are. Where, and when, we live will mould our thoughts. Some people flow with the current and others try to fight against it, no matter how futile the battle.

CUT TO

John Harvey Kellogg, an American doctor practicing in the early 1900s is one of these lone wolf Don Quixotes who fought a losing battle against, ahem, masturbation. To be fair, he was not the only one thinking sexual self-stimulation was detrimental at the time. A wave of prudishness had swept over the world and books with titles like *Ononia: Or the Heinous Sin of Self-Pollution* and *Treatise on the Diseases Produced by Onanism* were published to build public awareness of masturbation's many dangers. Kellogg – who abstained from sex his entire life for fear of its adverse effects on body and soul – was intent on finding a solution and came up with the idea of a healthy diet. If some foods acted as aphrodisiacs then there must surely be others that inhibited the libido. While working at a health retreat in Michigan, he experimented with oatmeal and corn to create a breakfast staple he called "granula", later changed to "granola". One of the tools he used was a roller that would turn grains into long sheets of dough. Whilst operating this roller one day, Kellogg left the dough to dry for a while and when he later tried to roll it, the kernels would snap off as flattened flakes instead of becoming a long, smooth paste. He tried baking the flakes instead of the dough and found the resulting cereal delicious. He named them Corn Flakes and it became the keystone for the company he formed with his brother Will Keith, W.K., Kellogg in 1906. While he did not succeed in his quest to stop masturbation, he created the world's most famous breakfast cereal.

Believing in the wrong things can produce useful results. The alchemists – the medieval forefathers of scientists – dreamt about creating The Philosopher's Stone, which would enable them to turn any material into any other material, most famously lead into gold. One of the hypotheses alchemists believed in was that materials sharing similar qualities must also share qualities deep down. For example, if two things shimmered like silver, it must mean they both contain silver. The hypothesis led alchemists to believe that urine, with its yellow colour, must contain traces of gold and so urine therefore became a key ingredient in many experiments of which the most famous was boiling the pee down to a white paste that glowed in the dark. They named the material *phosphorous*, "light-bringing" in Latin, and it became the thirteenth element ever discovered. Phosphorous would go on to become a significant ingredient in fertilizer, carbonated soft drinks and rust removal. The hypothesis that gold could be produced from urine strikes us as preposterous, yet the misconception produced a groundbreaking, practical insight.

Contrarianism

Being on a silly crusade – like alchemists and John Kellogg were – can spawn useful ideas. Another indication of the fact that ideas are products of their surroundings – as opposed to an isolated, individual insight – is when creators go against the mainstream, zigging instead of zagging.

CUT TO

Kevin Eastman and Peter Laird, two comic book artists working late one evening in 1983. This was a time when action comics were big business. *He-Man, GI Joe, Transformers* and *Star Wars* were all created by big companies selling cookie-cutter stories of heroes and villains. Laird and Eastman decided to go against the tide. They blended concepts from the bestselling comic books at the time: Mutants from Marvel's *X-Men*, teenage protagonists from virtually any comic and ninjas from *Daredevil*, another Marvel superhero. Instead of making the teenage mutant ninjas into humans, they made them masked turtles as a joke. In fact, inspired by Disney cartoons, they turned all the heroes and villains into various animals and, in another fit of contrarianism, they did not use common American first names for the turtles – Johnny, Rob, Dave, and so on – but named them after famous Renaissance artists; Raphael, Donatello, Leonardo and Michelangelo. The idea was just to have fun, and create something edgier than the homogenous comics at newsstands. Eastman and Laird self-published their creation and Teenage Mutant Ninja Turtles went on to became a pop culture phenomenon over the next couple of decades. The big companies that inspired these anti-heroes adapted the turtles for family-friendly Saturday morning cartoons and merchandise. What had been inspired by the mainstream to become something edgy and different slowly became the mainstream itself.

Make a Tool

There is a proverb amongst technology enthusiasts, originally attributed to science fiction author William Gibson, that the street finds its own uses for technology

– think DJs inventing scratching by moving turntables back and forth and making a musical instrument out of a playback machine. This way of creating things has become the norm in this age of digital entrepreneurship when the dream of any creator is for their idea to go viral and explode on to the screens of millions of users. The ease with which ideas spread today makes us think that this kind of viral distribution is a new phenomenon, which is not the case. New words, for example, are coined and then released into a population where they can take on a life of their own to become a part of everyday language.

CUT TO:

Paul Niquette, aged 19, programming a SWAC* Computer at UCLA in 1953, when it was one of only 16 machines in the entire United States. "Computer" was not the actual name used, as the word denoted a person who worked with computing numbers. The name Niquette and the other programmers used at the time was "giant brain", which is why the storage capacity was referred to as memory. "Brain" was a generous term since the only thing these big, heavy boxes could do was consume vast amounts of energy until a programmer came along to give the SWACs a set of routines and commands for them to perform. The idea that the commands could be taken

---

* The Standards Western Automatic Computer was a big, heavy machine that had approximately 256 words of memory using 2,300 vacuum tubes

from one machine and put into another was inconceivable at the time. One day, Niquette had an epiphany – a phlogiston moment – and a word popped into his head: "software". The behemoth machines he programmed had been referred to as hardware, a general term at the time describing any kind of machinery and "hardware stores" had been around for decades. "Software" sounded like a joke and as Niquette was known as a prankster around the UCLA campus, people initially laughed at the word. Niquette even described the word as a "throwaway thing". Fast-forward half a century and it is difficult to imagine the world without "software". What happened? How can a "throwaway" expression interpreted as a joke grow to infinite stature and significance? Most of us would probably assume it is simply a case of the word growing together with the rise of computing since the 1950s. This theory, however, is discarded when we look at the many words invented to describe computers around the same time: anatron, aptron, byter, cognitron, conteler, cortexer, cybertron, datatron, databyter, datajam, datawork, dynatron, flexidata, geobyte, heuritron, metabyter, maxibyter, novabyter, omnibyter, panatron, parabyter, polybyter, solutron, spectrabyter, synertron, trilobyter, velobyter, vitatron and xenobyter." Every single one of these words has been lost while "computer" survived, borrowed from what was then a profession for human beings, not machines.

Taking words from other areas is a convenient way to proceed in new inventions – the bicycle got its 'pedal' from the piano and the engine appropriated 'piston' from a trombone. For a word to spread, it must be simple enough for everyone to use and short enough to not waste human breath and effort every time we say it. This is why we do not say, "smoking an electronic cigarette" but instead refer to it as the two-syllable "vaping", thereby distinguishing it from traditional tobacco consumption. Similarly, many of the words to describe computers might simply have failed because they had too many syllables. The other requirement for a word to succeed is that the rules for language are written bottom-up. "Vaping" and "software" were not propositions by a governmental panel on language use ordered by decree to be used by the people. On the contrary, "software" was accidentally designed by Paul Niquette and people picked it up because they liked its design – it sounded funny – and found it simple and versatile enough to navigate a new area – computing. Like in product design, words need to be both useful and attractive. The street finds its own uses for technology, and words.

The Ecology of Creation

The 20th century has shifted our perception of artistic creation away from the lone genius to what music producer Brian Eno, the inventor of "ambient music", calls "scenius." Whereas "genius" describes a person with divine talent who creates in isolation, "scenius" describes the creative intelligence of a group of people working alongside each other. *We*-deas instead of *I*-deas. For this kind of collective creativity to emerge, however, the group needs to have some kind of meaningful diversity. If members are too like-minded, you get a sect. If they are too diverse, you have constant conflict. What is needed is a kind of *progressive friction* wherein the tensions and conflict within the meaningfully diverse group contribute to something greater.

CUT TO

Depeche Mode, an English music quartet, recording an album in a remote part of northern Denmark. It is the late 1980s and the group have for this, their seventh album, changed their writing process. For their earlier efforts, the main songwriter Martin Gore has come in with nearly finished compositions. Now, he has instead brought mere sketches – primitive demo tapes of him singing with either an organ or a guitar in the background. One of these sketches is a downbeat ballad called *Enjoy The Silence*. The rest of the group consists of lead singer David Gahan, keyboard player Alan Wilder and group mascot Andrew Fletcher. Their personalities could not be more different, with Gore as the tortured introvert, Gahan as the flamboyant frontman, Wilder as the pragmatic sound wizard and Fletcher mainly being in the band because the others like having him around. When they listen to Gore's demo tape, Wilder suggests, much to Gore's dismay, that they turn *Enjoy The Silence* into a disco song.

This adds a level of tension in the group that can either work to the detriment of the recording process or, if it is handled correctly, add magic to it. Wilder proceeds to find an old-school 1970s disco beat, think *Staying Alive* by *The Bee Gees*. Since they are in the remote Danish countryside with very few things to interfere with the recording process, they pass the time and ease the boredom by experimenting with new kinds of musical instruments. One of the machines is a brand new, state of the art modular synthesizer called Roland 700 series. Modular basically means that it consists of a keyboard and many boxes with plenty of knobs and buttons to fiddle around with – perfect for boredom alleviation in the Danish countryside. After playing around with the synthesizer for a while, they find a really interesting bass sound to go along with the disco beat. Martin Gore is continuously hostile to the way his precious, moody ballad is turned into a disco inferno so when the group asks him to produce a melody to go along with the rhythm, he proceeds to hammer away with the most irritating sound he can find on a keyboard. It would have been easy for the others to dismiss his behaviour as immature and ignore his shenanigans. Instead, Alan Wilder hears something within the random noise – a melody. He asks Gore to play it on a guitar instead, something Gore vehemently protests against since Depeche Mode are a synth band. When he finally strums the melody on a retro electric guitar, Depeche Mode have composed one of the most iconic songs in their career and their most successful hit single to this date. The tension between the individuals – primarily Wilder and Gore – translated into a song that is defined by its straddling of the melancholy and the upbeat, between major and minor chords.

Progressive friction can generate magic but is a fragile process. Alan Wilder would record one more album with Depeche Mode and then leave the band feeling betrayed, wounded and disillusioned. The albums of Depeche Mode would never sound as exciting again nor would they reach the career highs of the music they made with him in the band.

The Lost Mission

The music industry seems particularly adept at creating the conditions necessary to generate the small, wild ideas this book focuses on. To understand why, we need to look at how the rest of the business world has, to a certain extent, lost its mission. What was once a world of tinkering individuals and small companies has been transformed into giant corporations with stock prices to inflate and market shares to protect. What was once a thriving scene of homemade experiments has turned into legislation, red tape and risk management. A person experimenting with explosive material in his home today, like John Walker did when he invented matches, would likely get arrested and accused of being a terrorist.

Peter Thiel, a technology investor, argues that the reason we do not see exciting engineering projects like we did with nuclear power in the 1950s or the space missions of the 1970s is that governments manage everything from building projects to chemicals engineering in order to avoid the kind of free experimentation that was once mainstream. This spirit lives on in the music industry and in the kind of entrepreneurial businesses we see in the digital world. Furthermore, the music industry is at the confluence of many different forces. It is culture and commerce. It is about individuals sharing their most intimate thoughts or feelings but then being forced to work together with other people and reach out to connect with an audience. It is about heritage and renewal. Given the ability of the music industry to transform itself in the digital age, it is quite possibly one of the most interesting areas to learn from and emulate, whether your job is at a hospital, in a school, as a plumber, or as a writer.

Finally, and most interestingly given the topic of this book, artistic creation often has a blatant disregard for goals, objectives and strategies – the things that hold businesses to a beaten path and get in the way of exploration. The next chapter will look more closely at what happens when this kind of travelling without a map is put into practice.

CHAPTER

9

BLISSFUL IGNORANCE

CUT TO

The winter of 1913 and a group of struggling artists have organized a charity auction to help the impoverished poet Else Lasker-Schuler. Unfortunately, the auction was a failure and the artists were forced to bid for each other's work, raising only a tiny amount. When German author Florian Illies wrote about the incident a hundred years later, he commented that "the total value of the works unsold [at the failed auction in] February 1913 would amount to around 100 million Euros today." There are many examples like this, of snubbed artists, overlooked masterpieces and missed opportunities and we love hearing about them because it makes us feel smart, like if we had been there, we would have done things differently. This is a thrilling thought but a misleading one, because the owl of Minerva flies only at dusk. This philosophic statement from Friedrich Hegel needs some explanation. "Minerva" is the Roman name for the Greek Athena, goddess of wisdom and philosophy. The meaning of Hegel's saying is that philosophy and wisdom take flight only at the end of the day, after the main events have taken place. There is, in other words, no predictive power in philosophy, much as we would all like to have bid at the 1913 auction, or convince that infamous record company executive that signing the Beatles would be a good idea. We yearn for recipes for success – how to make it in life, in love and in our careers – and forget a logical fallacy called "post hoc ergo propter hoc" (literally "afterwards, therefore because of"). This fallacy makes us believe that if we only repeat everything somebody successful has done in sequence, we too would be blessed with that success. According to this kind of logic, if we all drove drunk tonight, we would invent the Whopper and if we fed herbicides to sick children, we would invent Orfadin. This kind of prescriptive approach to innovation is highly questionable yet understandable since there is something reassuring in recipes: all we need to do is add x to y and success is ours. The opposite view, possibly closer to reality, is more unnerving; things happen only once and we are alone in the quest to explore what works. This chapter will look closer at some people who walked this lonely path, poking around for answers with no exact idea of where to go.

CUT TO

Young entrepreneur Hjalmar Winbladh sweeping a staircase in a suburb of Stockholm in the late 1980s. He started a cleaning company right out of high school to satisfy an entrepreneurial urge, possibly inherited from his paternal grandfather who had imported the lunch tray to Sweden from America in the 1950s. Winbladh's small company focused mainly on sweeping the staircases of apartment blocks and office buildings, which gave him the idea for his next company. He observed that very common daytime users of staircases were couriers, who would pick up and drop off parcels at various companies. Winbladh did some research about the

courier companies and found a lucrative, yet fragmented and uncoordinated industry taking shape in
Stockholm. Most couriers were one-man outfits featuring couriers who mainly got into it for the love of fast
cars, or motorcycles. The lack of coordination meant that
many cars drove empty in the suburbs after or before
they had dropped off a parcel or picked one up. What
if this waste of space could be resolved somehow? The
main users of courier services in the 1980s were advertising agencies, so Winbladh decided to focus his efforts
on them. He created a new kind of courier company
which used cooler cars, nicer-looking staff – to woo the
advertising agency receptionists – and Hollywood style
parties to add a sense of glamour. Most importantly, to
coordinate the pick-ups and drop-offs, Winbladh built
a crude piece of software to connect cars to a central
dispatch, a mobile messaging service of sorts. This was
before ubiquitous mobile phones and SMS text messag-
es so Winbladh's couriers would often drive with a large
portable computer in the glove compartment and use
noisy analogue modems. After a few years, his fascina-
tion with the technology platform became greater than
his interest for courier services, so he started to envision
selling the technology to parcel handlers in other cities
around the world. Surely the companies serving the advertising agencies of London and New York would have
a great interest in this kind of advantage and deeper
pockets too. Winbladh discovered this was not the case.
In fact, it was a bit like selling a space station to a cave
man. His global road show to sell technology licenses

rendered only two takers, both of which went bankrupt within a year.

Disappointed, he went to CeBIT, a German technology exhibition, and learned about something called The World Wide Web. He describes it as an epiphany – another phlogiston moment – when he realized that the future of mobility was connecting the analogue with the digital world. He started outlining a world where our email would be our identity and the internet would be in your pocket. He sold off the courier part of the business and kept the messaging service. It was a huge gamble that left him in debt and had his bank threaten to repossess his house. His first customer was a small Swedish telecom operator who wanted to be perceived as an innovative pioneer and offer customers the very latest kind of messaging service. This was during a time when the telecom industry was in transition and state-owned incumbents were competing with start-ups to grab market share. Based on this first contract, Winbladh was able to sell his technology throughout the world by using the sly argument: "Your competitor has taken an interest in this." Business was picking up and soon enough, he counted some of the biggest telecom operators in the world as his clients so his company had to work long hours to meet deadlines. He had, however, made a crucial mistake: he had based his technology on a Microsoft Windows platform that was slow, cumbersome and hard to scale. It frustrated him to a point where he ended up going to Microsoft's headquarters in Redmond and basically yelled at the staff, calling the software a "bag of shit." Impressed with Winbladh's drive and his company's growth, Microsoft bought his company. The lesson? Sweeping floors in a Swedish suburb can make you a billionaire.

Life happens when we make other plans

What the case of Hjalmar Winbladh – and that of many other entrepreneurs - illustrates is the benefits of navigating without a rigid plan. Winbladh had a vague notion – that the world of messaging would become increasingly digital and mobile – but his strength was not his visionary acumen, but his agility and reacting quickly to new stimuli. He kept reacting to opportunities and challenges to propel him in a new direction. We can call this ability *pinballing*, if you envision the silver ball of a pinball machine being knocked about, changing direction and always heading somewhere new and unexpected. Pinballing is more important – and more rewarding – than rigid planning.

CUT TO

A young Italian man turning a salad bowl upside down to invent the modern kitchen lamp. Fratelli Guzzini, a family-owned kitchen utensils company located in Recanati, Italy, with a long, rich history of innovation. In 1938, the company began to use the scrap from cut

Plexiglas sheets to produce windows for military planes, as Italian industry was ordered to be a part of the war effort. The moulding technology was similar to that used by the company to transform ox horn into cutlery, tableware and cigarette cases. After the Second World War, with Italy on the losers' side, the next generation of heirs of Fratelli Guzzini went a step further. Having learnt the techniques of Plexiglas sheet moulding, they acquired a patent to transform Plexiglas scrap into a new raw material. This allowed them to produce sheets of whatever size and colour they needed to make tableware – glasses, cutlery and plates. The modern design and colours of these objects soon became the foundation for the kind of plastic tableware the company is still known for.

Years pass and yet another generation of heirs came along and saw the opportunity to broaden production by adding Plexiglas lamps to the company's distinctive tableware products. They used the concave shapes of salad bowls to create a large pendant lamp that became a common kitchen feature across Europe and laid the foundation for what is today one of the most successful lightning fixture companies in the world, iGuzzini. The name even preceded Apple's appropriation of the lower case "i" by decades. Turning a salad bowl upside down created the modern kitchen lamp.

The birth of iGuzzini illustrates not only the merits of pinballing but also the hidden value of residuals – waste products, in this case Plexiglas scrap. Sometimes we do something only to discover that what was valuable was not the thing we focus on but things happening on the side. The experimentation with coal tar – a messy waste product of coal – in the early 1800s gave birth not only to synthetic, cheap dyes for the fashion industry, but also to saccharine, explosives, antiseptics, and cosmetics.

A deer stuck in the headlights of tomorrow

Chapter Six argued that having a path can transform random blips to meaningful bings and this can easily create some confusion with this chapter's examples of map-less journeys. What distinguishes a path from a map? The answer is that a path has soft edges whereas a map has firm ones. When we look for directions on a map, we do not want blurry lines or ambiguous signals. Yet a map is not an accurate reflection of the territory, just a simplification designed for clarity.

English poet Sir Stephen Spender said it well: "The greatest of all human delusions is that there is a tangible goal." This delusion has become an addiction in the 21st century. Self-help books, financial planners and management gurus urge us to set goals and work diligently to make them come true. Goals are a valuable planning tool when the outcome is binary and easy to visualize, like arriving at point x on a map. The messy, contradictory and uncertain future is rarely like this. Setting goals, finding convictions and sticking to plans can hinder more than help us.

CUT TO

Film director Quentin Tarantino is having an informal lunch with fellow filmmaker Luc Besson in the late
2000s. Tarantino, who had just experienced his first failure at the box office with the movie *Death Proof*, was
planning to take a step back from the silver screen and
release his next project – *Inglourious Basterds* (sic) – as
a TV series. Most people he had shared this plan with
complimented him and said it was the right way forward. Besson, being a contrarian Frenchman, stayed silent as Tarantino shared his idea and then said: "You're
one of the few directors that I actually like to leave the
house for to go see your movies at the theatres. And
now you're telling me I'm going to have to wait years
to do that? I'm a little disappointed." Tarantino refers
to this moment as pivotal: "You can't unhear it … it
was running around in my head. So I said [to myself],
'Let me try and turn this into a movie one more time.'"
He did and *Inglourious Basterds* became one of Tarantino's finest accomplishments artistically and biggest
successes commercially.

Many self-help books and management gurus would
frown upon Tarantino's change of heart and call it
flip-flopping. Even bringing this example up is somewhat dishonest since it describes a change of heart that
ultimately had a positive outcome. What if *Inglourious
Basterds* had failed? Would we still see the flip-flopping
as positive? Probably not. Yet what this book argues is

that there are no recipes for success – only stories about what has worked in the past. These stories are not guidelines but catalysts to a different way of thinking. The key is not to veer off of one path – like making a TV series – because another is more alluring – or because Luc Besson said so – but because you are open to the prospect that your convictions might be wrong. They say that a fanatic is somebody who cannot change his mind and will not change the subject. What we need is the opposite of fanaticism, where changing your mind is a key to openness, not a source of ridicule. This chapter's final story will illustrate how easy opportunities are lost when we stubbornly stick to plans and heuristics.

CUT TO

Swedish film director Ulf Malmros being handed a 500-page book manuscript by a friend in the early 2000s.

"Read it!" the friend urges, "It is a detective story by some unknown journalist. No publishers have picked it up, but I think it would make for a great movie."

Malmros feigns mild interest to conceal the fact that he has no intention of reading it. The manuscript, in a raggedy old binder, sets off all the warning bells for him: unknown journalist, no publisher interest and a detective story, the intellectual gutter amongst genres. He lets the binder sit on a shelf at home for a few weeks and then gives it back without even opening it.

He would come to regret this.

The unknown journalist was Stieg Larsson and the manuscript was *The Girl With The Dragon Tattoo*. The book would go on to sell 15 million copies worldwide and spawn a series of movies including a big budget Hollywood film by director David Fincher. Be careful what you say no to. The demons that torment us – failure, uncertainty and doubt – might actually be angels sent to open our eyes.

A world without leadership

We yearn for a leader. Traditional, rational or charismatic matters less as long as that special somebody can come and lift us up, show us the way and inspire us to greatness. We have been taught that the opposite of leadership is something negative – like a micro-managing boss or a spineless follower. What if there is a desirable antonym to "leader"? Somebody guided not by convictions but by doubt, scepticism and an openness to experiment? What should we call such a person? This book has named many of them – from British pop groups to Swedish doctors – but not offered a useful collective description of what it is these people practice. How about calling it *Sanscontourism* – from the French description of being without contours, boundaries? Because if there is one thing that unites these stories, it is the insight that the human mind truly knows no boundaries. Between important and unimportant, between right and wrong, between East and West and between good and bad. We can be taught to distinguish between them but there are no built-in mechanisms in the brain.

This is both a flaw and a blessing. It explains the number of zealots in the world with bad, destructive ideas about what will bring them into paradise. It explains historical revisionism and conspiracy theories. Yet it also explains how a musician in Idaho can get inspired by rhythms composed in Ghana. Or how a failed herbicide can save lives. *Sanscontourism* is what makes life unpredictable and the future forever blurry. It is also a source of optimism.

CONCLUSION – THE UNSEEN

CUT TO

Me waking up early one morning in August 2005.

There is a warm feeling inside of me unlike anything I have felt before. It is like a whisper and a presence and a comforting hug all at once.

I have been wasting my time in a dead-end job for a few years but been too afraid to quit.

The feeling tells me that it is time to break up, move on and start a new journey.

I was petrified and had no idea what I would do with my life. I was 31 years old, had just proposed to my fiancé and needed money for our upcoming wedding. Quitting my job was not exactly the best step to take. It never is. I did it anyway and have never regretted it.

So what happened that morning in 2005? Had we put a video camera in the room it would have looked like nothing – just some random person waking up in an un-remarkable bedroom.

Yet it was real to me.

The feeling and its consequences.

What do we do about the things we cannot see, touch or even describe?

"The most beautiful thing we can experience is the mysterious. It is the source of all true art and science. He to whom the emotion is a stranger, who can no longer pause to wonder and stand wrapped in awe, is as good as dead – his eyes are closed", as Albert Einstein said.

The famous architect Frank Lloyd Wright liked telling a story from his childhood in which he was crossing a field in the snow with his uncle. When they reached the other side, Lloyd Wright saw that the uncle's tracks were straight, whereas his own were wandering in a seemingly random zigzag between the fence, the cattle, to the woods and back again. He determined right then "not to miss the most important things in life, as my uncle had." He attributes this curiosity and love of mystery as the most important contribution to his work in architecture and his vision for design.

This final chapter of the book will reflect on what it is to live in a world full of unseen, often inexplicable things.

Living with Mystery

The British philosopher Alan Watts said, "The universe is a giant Rorschach ink-blot. Science finds one meaning in it in the 18th century, another in the 19th, a third in the 20th; each artist finds unique meanings on other levels of abstraction; and each man and woman finds different meanings at different hours of the day, depending on the internal and external environments."

What really happened when Rod Stewart blessed Jens Spendrup's investment in Lowenbrau or when James McLamore drove drunk on a Florida highway?

What happened to me that morning in 2005?

The slightly unsettling answer is that we might never know. These are one-off events – a data point of only one observation to express it in scientific terms – and forming any kind of conclusion from one-off events is not only difficult but possibly deceptive.

Events that triggered something big – from Gavrilo Princip assassinating archduke Franz Ferdinand in 1914 to Charles Stewart Rolls and Frederick Henry Royce meeting by chance in a Manchester hotel and later creating the company Rolls-Royce – take on mythical proportions because they look like they are part of a celestial master plan. This is why we have such a loud, heated debate about the world we live in right now – we want to find a pattern that reveals a path and explains whether the world will become paradise over the coming century... or hell. We went from being an experimental place that anyone could join to seeing the world as a spectator sport where big ideas do battle with us as its pawns and victims.

Just as nature abhors a vacuum, people hate mystery and the feeling of not knowing. We would rather be convinced by the wrong idea than left hovering in uncertainty by complexity. Imagine someone who is looking out at the world and feels a deep sense of unease and looming disaster. He is afraid that his country will be overwhelmed by alien races, afraid of what American technology is capable of, afraid of big cities, uncontrolled industrialization, the economization of everything and the moral debasement of art. These are worries many of us might share in the 2010s yet the person described here is Adolf Hitler in the 1920s, as described by the German biographer Joachim Fest.

To worry is human, but to let the worries translate into divisive, destructive rhetoric is our own choice. When we let our convictions be guided by fear or, to put it another way, when our fears harden into convictions, we are bound to make disastrous choices in life.

The Lost Lesson (We Need to Relearn)

Imagine remaking the story of how Orfadin was created – the failed herbicide that saved terminally ill children – for the 21st century. Imagine we are Hollywood producers intending to create an award-winning drama about the struggle of two doctors in the face of impossible odds. We would have to change certain things to accommodate a changing world. First of all, we cannot have Dr Elisabeth Holme smoking as it sends a bad message and has since been proven even more detrimental to people's health. Secondly, it is unlikely that any company today would document its failures the way Zeneca did in the 1980s. But we can create a character that stands up for the right to do "good science" and who wants the world to know why the herbicide failed. Thirdly – and here we run into a serious problem – very few hospitals would approve of feeding a failed herbicide to sick children today. For the general public to hear about a terminally ill child dying of her disease is sad but for them to hear about a child dying because two rogue doctors fed her poison is an outrage and a PR disaster. Hospital staff would lose their jobs. There might even be death threats.

We used to be more relaxed about the question "What if?" and even slightly optimistic when we pondered tomorrow's possibilities.

These days, we are prone to worry and think in terms of worst possible outcome.

This is why voices, afraid of offending someone, remain silent.

We sacrifice the future on the altar of fear.

Reclaim The Future

What this book has set out to show is that innovations and discoveries can – and will – come from anywhere, anyone at any time. We do not need large, expensive innovation departments and cumbersome processes, only our willingness to explore the world around us – whether it is a divine hamburger in Jacksonville or the thinnest carbon residue on a piece of tape.

Friedrich Hayek, a famous economist, said, "The curious task of economics is to demonstrate to men how little they really know about what they imagine they can design." The modern economy is a transformational reallocation machine. To get food, most of us don't grow food or keep livestock, we write computer code, clean hospital corridors, wait tables or service cars. When the powers that be urge us to believe in a singular idea or rally behind one important cause, it does the economy a disservice. If everyone believed in the same thing, it would be a poor world, not a rich one. Plurality – even when it appears as disagreement and debate – is a cause for optimism.

Every moment has its secrets, a chance to turn it all around.

Everything is important. Nothing is redundant.

In the words of musician Nick Cave:

"All of our days are numbered. We cannot afford to be idle. To act on a bad idea is better than to not act at all because the worth of the idea never becomes apparent until you do it. Sometimes this idea can be the smallest thing in the world; a little flame that you hunch over and cup with your hand and pray will not be extinguished by all the storm that howls about it. If you can hold on to that flame, great things can be constructed around it; things that are massive and powerful and world changing. All held up by the tiniest of ideas."

The sun is setting on the alpine slopes in Davos and the snow is yet again turning blue.

We live in times where a lot of people like to use these five words: "We live in times of …"

Don't be a slave to other people's ideas about the future. Create your own.

CHAPTER

THE MINIFESTO

1. **The Future Does Not Exist**

   The idea that there is a fixed destination called The Future waiting for us on the other side of the timeline is an illusion conjured up by the brain. There is no future, only tinkering people working in organizations, in basements, garages and laboratories. If we fall for the illusion of The Future, we will make plans and calculate probabilities. If we leave this illusion behind, we will plan for adventures, make gambles, experiment and travel to get lost, not arrive. Let us stop admiring the things we have made and start dreaming of the things we have not. Ideas can change the world, but most ideas change nothing while many just change small things.

2. **We are Alchemists of Creation**

   We do not know why some things work and others don't. We can guess, hypothesise and storify, but this does not hide the fact that we are like the alchemists once were, making it all up as we go along. There are no recipes; a recipe is merely an instruction manual for repeating the past, whether it is baking a cupcake or building a company. There are only sparks. We should embrace the path of a faithless alchemist. When we let go of our beliefs, we liberate our creative spark. When we lose the past, the future reveals itself inside of us.

3. **Seek to hunt for Wild Ideas**

   Be brave and go where others do not. As author Hunter S. Thompson once said: "Yesterday's weirdness is tomorrow's reason why." Fashion is beautiful today but ugly tomorrow while art is ugly today but may be beautiful tomorrow. Pet ideas are cute and seek agreement. Wild ideas can grow anywhere and look like nothing. Big ideas are a perfect excuse to get nothing done. "Don't try to change the world, that's a concept floating on our horizon. Just use your wits and change your heads", as artist and composer Yoko Ono urged us.

4. **Find your Muzone**

   Do not believe in the myth that life is elsewhere and that creation resides in all things Silicon Valley. Within you lies a deep well of inspiration called The Muzone and only you hold the keys to its unlocking. Some unlock it through silence, others through noise. Some need to be where people are to get in touch with this inner muse, whilst others climb high up on a lonely mountain to hear it.

5. **Life is full of Phlogiston**

   Suddenly, something clicks into place and you see it all clearly. There is no reason why, it just happens then and there. The alchemists thought of Phlogiston as a mysterious combustible element hidden inside other materials when what they were really describing was a moment when doubt, mystery and experimentation came together to produce something unexpected, interesting and sometimes even magnificent.

6. **Behold The Moments of Mutation!**

   Embrace the peculiarities that make you go "hmmm." As science-fiction author Isaac Asimov said: "The most exciting phrase to hear in science, the one that heralds new discoveries, is not 'Eureka' but 'That's funny...'"

7. **Observation!**

   Seek newledge, not knowledge. Ignore luck, chance, serendipity and accidents – what happens around us is of lesser importance, what you see in these events is all that matters. Moments of mutation, rich in phlogiston, are really portals of discovery if we let them be. Play. Pay attention to the invisible. Marvel over everything, especially the most ordinary things.

8. **Embrace Progressive Friction**

   Do not seek the deceptive embrace of agreement – this is a fleeting moment intended to minimise discomfort for all participants. All creation – from procreation to innovation – requires the friction of bodies, ideas, minds and visions colliding. Merely friction is not enough – it needs rips and tears. Progressive friction rips, tears and builds anew. Create meaningful diversity where differences gel together like pieces in a puzzle, albeit a jagged, difficult puzzle.

9. **Pinball!**

   Life is a series of lost futures and we become the experiments that did not fail. We should try out all kinds of futures – will this career suit me? What if I add sugar or salt into the mix? Like trying on a new shoe or leather jacket, the initial feeling will be one of slight discomfort as you are unaccustomed to the new garment. You have no idea what will work, but if you try it on and you feel something within the discomfort, a silent promise of a different tomorrow, you are surely on to something useful. Do not plan too heavily but bounce off opportunities and failures, like a pinball, forever forward.

10. **Stay Free!**

    Before "freedom to", we need "freedom from". Before we can experiment and explore, we need to lose the shackles of The Seceity – the roar of voices that demands of us to choose sides. Creation thrives in openness where we are free from and free to. We should practice sanscontourism, the opposite of leadership, which asks of us to live in doubts, mysteries and vulnerability. A fixed salary hinders creative thinking as it enslaves us to do what it required, not what is interesting.

SOURCES

Introduction Chapter

"In pharmaceutical research, of the drugs approved by the United States Federal Drug Administration..." taken from Hurley, Dan. "Why Are So Few Blockbuster Drugs Invented Today?" *New York Times*, November 13, 2014.

Chapter 1: Blanket-bombed by Blah-blah

Jaron Lainier's quote is taken from Khatchadourian, Raffi. "The Doomsday Invention." *The New Yorker*, November 23, 2015.

Chapter 2: Welcome to The Seceity

The insight about Monster energy drinks and its details taken from Krantz, Matt. "This isn't your father's Nasdaq." *USA Today*, March 2, 2015.

Chapter 3: The Moment of Creation

The description of alchemy is taken from Ball, Philip. "A shared secret?" *Chemistry World*, August 26, 2015.

Chapter 4: The Difference Between Ideas and Ideas

The metaphor of sunflowers and bougainvillea is taken from Heller, Nathan. "Listen and Learn." *The New Yorker*, July 9, 2012.

The idea of traveling to arrive or travelling to get lost
was taken from Rowland Smith, Robert. "Beyond Ideas."
Lecture at The Royal Society for the encouragement of Arts,
Manufactures and Commerce, London, July 17, 2015.

The concept of "Is the World flat or a Mountain?" was
developed by Peter Thiel and retrieved from the lecture
notes of his course at Stanford University in 2012. Masters,
Blake. "Peter Thiel's CS183: Startup - Class 3 Notes Essay",
http://blakemasters.com/post/20955341708/peter-thiels-cs183-
startup-class-3-notes-essay retrieved on December 3, 2015.

Chapter 5: Failureology

All information about Jens Spendrup from personal interview
conducted on December 4, 2015.

Jens Spendrup is adamant that everything he did to build his
company was done in a close relationship with his brother
Ulf. This example is therefore dedicated to both of them.

The story about Mattel and Masters of the Universe is taken
from Harris, Blake. "How Did This Get Made: Masters of the
Universe (An Oral History)." Slashfilm.com, October 2, 2015.
http://www.slashfilm.com/masters-of-the-universe-oral-history/
retrieved on October 2, 2015.

The story of Frank Sinatra taken from Gradvall, Jan.
"Omstart: Hur man överlever sitt inre Finspång och kommer
ut starkare på andra sidan." *Dagens Industri*, May 12, 2014.
And "How did Frank Sinatra really get the role of Maggio
in From Here to Eternity?" Examiner.com, July 21, 2010.

http://www.examiner.com/article/how-did-frank-sinatra-really-get-the-role-of-maggio-from-here-to-eternity retrieved on December 30, 2015.

The story about U2 and all quotes are taken from *From The Sky Down*, Davis Guggenheim. Documentary Partners, 2011.

Robert Rowland Smith's quote is taken from from Rowland Smith, Robert. "Beyond Ideas." Lecture at The Royal Society for the encouragement of Arts, Manufactures and Commerce, London, July 17, 2015.

Chapter 6: Souvenirs From The Great Beyond

The anecdote about James McLamore and the Whopper is taken from McLamore, James W. *The Burger King*. Mcgraw-Hil, 1997.
However, a *mea culpa* is in order here since James McLamore wasn't actually driving the car when under the influence. This was discovered when I finally got my hands on the book itself having relied on a second-hand retelling of the book until that point.

Sam Harris insights are taken from Harris, Sam. "Drugs and the Meaning of Life." *Waking up with Sam Harris*. Podcast Audio. July 4, 2011. https://www.samharris.org/podcast/item/drugs-and-the-meaning-of-life

John Seabrook's quote is taken from Seabrook, John. *Song Machine*. W. W. Norton & Company, 2015.

The story about Amy Winehouse is from *Amy*, Asif Kapadia. Film 4, 2015.

The story about the invention of Orfadin is taken from Lock et al, "From toxological problem to therapeutic use", *Journal of Inherited Metabolic Disease*, August 1998, Volume 21, Issue 5 and personal interview with with Sirkka Thomé, SOBI, November 28, 2015. She also generously supplied materials.

The description of obliquity is from Kay, John. "Obliquity." Johnkay.com, 17 January 2004. Retrieved on December 30, 2015.

The story of Swiss watch making is taken from Reddick, Max E. "John Calvin's Austerity and the Birth of the Swiss Watch Industry." Monochrome-watches.com, November 13, 2011, retrieved on November 20, 2015.
And Thompson, Clive. "Can the Swiss Watchmaker Survive the Digital Age?" *The New York Times*, June 3, 2015.

Chapter 7: Seeing What Could Be

The story of John Walker is taken from "Accident plays role in many inventions." *Smithsonian Magazine*, September 2, 2003.

Cesar Hidalgo's insight and quote are taken from Hidalgo, Cesar. *Why Information Grows*. Basic Books, 2015.

The story of Brian Eno is taken from https://en.wikipedia.org/wiki/Discreet_Music retrieved on December 30, 2015

The story of Andre Geim is taken from Colapinto, John. "Material Question." *New Yorker*. December 22 & 29, 2014.

The quote from Peter Dinklage is taken from Kois, Dan. "Peter Dinklage Was Smart to Say No." *The New York Times*, March 29, 2012.

The story of the Slinky is taken from Warner, Andy. "How a Naval Engineer Turned a Torsion Spring into the Slinky. "Backchannel.com, June 23, 2015. https://backchannel. com/how-a-naval-engineer-turned-a-torsion-spring-into-the-slinky-977877664f2d#.ezfrp83wy retrieved on September 8, 2015.

The story of Alberto "Beto" Perez is taken from Mendoza-Dayrit, Mylene. "How Beto Perez invented the Zumba." *The Philippine Star*, May 21, 2013.

The story of Ace of Base is taken from Seabrook, John. *Song Machine*. W. W. Norton & Company, 2015

Chapter 8 : We-deas

The story about Michael Buffer is taken from "Michael Buffer Interview - How it all started." YouTube video. Posted July 14, 2011. https://www.youtube.com/watch?v=44XNBpl7u2k

The story of Melitta Bentz is taken from https://en.wikipedia. org/wiki/Melitta_Bentz

Sources

The story about Corn Flakes is taken from Soniak, Matt. "Corn Flakes Were Invented as Part of an Anti-Masturbation Crusade." *Mental Floss*, December 28, 2012.

The story of urine and phosphorous is from "How Pee Brought You The Modern World." YouTube Video. Posted October 5, 2015. https://www.youtube.com/watch?v=BTFw5g0WzJ8

The story of Teenage Mutant Ninja Turtles is taken from Collins, Sean T. "How 'Teenage Mutant Ninja Turtles' Went From In-Joke to Blockbuster." *Rolling Stone*m, August 14, 2014.

The origin of the word "software" is taken from Niquette, Paul. "Introduction: The Software Age." Niquette.com, 1995. http://niquette.com/books/softword/part0.htm retrieved on January 23, 2016.

The quotes from Matt Ridley are taken from Frisby, Dominic. "Matt Ridley." *The Virgin Podcast*, Podcast audio. September 15, 2015. https://www.virgin.com/disruptors/the-virgin-podcast-matt-ridley
And
Ridley, Matt. *The Evolution of Everything*. Harper, 2015

The idea of "scenius" is described by Brian Eno at "Brian Eno On Genius, And "Scenius", Synthopia.com, July 9, 2009. http://www.synthtopia.com/content/2009/07/09/brian-eno-on-genius-and-scenius/ retrieved on October 12, 2015.

The story of Depeche Mode is taken from "FLOOD about the making of Enjoy the Silence @ Short Circuit Presents Mute festival." YouTube video. May 29, 2011. https://www.youtube.com/watch?v=dm2HM44aAJo&list=PLDw5oArniYUf-0G68fqd7DKhpqkxBQ9Kt

Chapter 9: Blissful Ignorance

Florian Illies book from which the art auction comes is called Illies, Florian. *1913: The Year Before the Storm*. Melville House, 2013.

The explanation of the owl of Minerva was provided by http://www.askphilosophers.org/question/1579

The story of Hjalmar Winbladh was provided by a personal interview conducted on December 14, 2015.

The story of iGuzzini was provided by a personal interview with Nicola Orlandi, November 28, 2014 and followed up by an email from Ceregioli Piergiovanni of iGuzzini in May 2015.

The anecdote about Quentin Tarantino is from *Director's Chair*. "Quentin Tarantino." Season 1, Episode 3. Directed by Robert Rodriguez. El Rey Network. Aired 14 August, 2014.

The anecdote about Ulf Malmros is from *Sommar i P1*. "Ulf Malmros." Swedish public radio P1. Aired July 4, 2010.

Chapter 10: Conclusion - The Unseen

The quote from Alan Watts is taken from Sterling, Bruce and Lebkowsky, Jon. "State of the World 2016." The Well. January 3, 2016. http://www.well.com/conf/inkwell.vue/topics/487/Bruce-Sterling-Jon-Lebkowsky-Sta-page01.html retrieved on January 3, 2016.

Joachim Fest's biography about Hitler is Fest, Joachim. *Hitler*. Harcourt Brace Jovanovich, 1974.

The Nick Cave quote is from *20,000 Days on Earth*. Directed by Iain Forsyth and Jane Pollard. Corniche Pictures, 2014.

AN INTRODUCTION TO
MAGNUS LINDKVIST

Magnus Lindkvist is a futurologist whose thinking
has inspired thousands around the world.
His previous books are:
*Everything We Know is Wrong: The Trendspotter's
Handbook* (2009)
*The Attack of The Unexpected: A Guide to Surprises
and Uncertainty* (2010)
*When The Future Begins: A Guide to Long-Term
Thinking* (2013)
And
*The Future Book: Forty Ways to Future-Proof
your Work and Life* (2015).

More information can be found on
magnuslindkvist.com